THE *Nightly*

POSI

QUOT

THE *Nightly* BOOK OF
POSITIVE
QUOTATIONS

By Steve Deger

Fairview Press
Minneapolis

Published by Fairview Press, 2450 Riverside Avenue, Minneapolis, Minnesota 55454. Fairview Press is a division of Fairview Health Services, a community-focused health system, affiliated with the University of Minnesota, providing a complete range of services, from the prevention of illness and injury to care for the most complex medical conditions.

For a free current catalog of Fairview Press titles, please call toll-free 1-800-544-8207. Or visit our Website at www.fairviewpress.org.

Library of Congress Cataloging-in-Publication Data
Deger, Steve, 1966-
 The nightly book of positive quotations / [compiled by] Steve Deger.
  p. cm.
 ISBN 978-1-57749-188-0 (pbk. : alk. paper) 1. Conduct of life—
Quotations, maxims, etc. 2. Inspiration—Quotations, maxims, etc.
3. Motivation (Psychology)—Quotations, maxims, etc. 4. Quotations,
English. I. Title.
 PN6084.C556D45 2009
 080—dc22

                                    2009014938

Interior design: Ryan Scheife, Mayfly Design (www.mayflydesign.net)
Printed in Canada
First Printing: July 2009
13 12 11 10   7 6 5 4 3 2

INTRODUCTION

Evening is meant for reflection. It's the time of day when we instinctively look back on what we've accomplished, and entertain new dreams for the future.

When we are comfortable with ourselves and content with our lives, such moments are full of magic and wonder. Looking back, we realize our values have led us on a path toward our goals and dreams. This path may have been a meandering one—chance encounters and unforeseen events often take each of us down some interesting "side trails." But, by following our hearts and a set of guiding principles, we eventually end up exactly where we were meant to be all along. Looking toward the future, we know there will be similar detours. Yet our faith bolsters our courage and allows us to embrace the mystery of whatever lies ahead.

Conversely—when we are struggling with physical, emotional, financial, or other issues—such reflective moments tend to be anything but peaceful and reassuring. These are the sleepless nights we spend filled with regret, doubt, and uncertainty. *Did I make a wrong turn somewhere along the way? Why can't I or my loved ones get out of this mess? Is this the best I can expect?*

The intent of this book is not to give you a map of this winding path, but rather to bathe the trail in moonlight, so you can find your own way.

Each night, you are invited to read a quotation and consider the discussion that follows. Do you agree or disagree? Is this a new outlook for you, or does it confirm something you already believe?

However you choose to use this book, the hope is that the wisdom you find here will help you find comfort and peace in your evening, so you may face tomorrow with a sense of hope and optimism.

The
Nightly Book
of
Positive Quotations

Open the gate

"The world is all gates, all opportunities, strings of tension waiting to be struck."

—⌇ RALPH WALDO EMERSON

Opportunity sometimes seems to knock more frequently on some people's doors, while others struggle, wondering when they'll get their big break. If we look closer, we see that lucky individuals share some traits. They expect to find opportunity around every corner. They can view any new situation, even a difficult one, as an opportunity.

The world is brimming with possibility. What if we were to enter each day and moment with an attitude of childlike curiosity? Look, here is another gate, a transition from one space to another. We reach out and lift the latch, hear the creak of the hinges, and, instead of staying where it is safe and familiar, we step through.

I resolve to open a new gate in my life. I'll take a peek and see what's on the other side.

Sound body, sound mind

" To keep the body in good health is a duty . . . otherwise we shall not be able to keep our mind strong and clear. "

—⌒ BUDDHA

When we don't take care of our physical health, problems can crop up. We find ourselves distracted by sickness, poor energy, and aches and pains. Keeping ourselves healthy is about more than avoiding the mental distraction of discomfort. The requirements of good physical health—nourishment, rest, movement—empower our minds, too. Creative thought, problem-solving, and a calm attitude are enhanced by the same actions that meet our physical needs.

If I'm too busy to care for my body, it will likely affect my thoughts, too. Taking the time to eat well and exercise will sharpen and strengthen my mind as well.

Cultivate friendship

"Go oft to the house of thy friend, for weeds choke the unused path."

— RALPH WALDO EMERSON

Our closest friends share our burdens and double our joys; their lives are deeply intertwined with our own. It takes time and kindness to cultivate and care for these relationships. What a joy it is to take that time! It is a reward in itself.

I am thankful for my friends. We have shared so many experiences, cares, and happiness. I will connect with one good friend and let them know how precious our relationship is.

I make my life rich

> *"To wait for someone else, or to expect someone else to make my life richer, or fuller, or more satisfying, puts me in a constant state of suspension."*
>
> —✦ KATHLEEN TIERNEY ANDRUS

We may believe in the fairy-tale ending: Someday an event or a special person will make us truly happy. Waiting for a nebulous happily-ever-after can leave us waiting forever, stuck in a state of wondering, "what if?" Opportunities remain undiscovered and new activities remain untried.

It's up to us to create the life of our dreams. Once we commit to that, our interactions with others and the gifts we happen upon can double the richness that was already there.

I don't have to wait for more money or time or someone else's action. There are small steps I can take to create a more satisfying life right now.

Persistent opportunity

"Opportunity knocks at every man's door once.
On some men's door, it hammers till it breaks
down the door, and then it goes in and wakes him
up if he's asleep, and ever afterward it works for
him as a night watchman."

—⌐ FINLEY PETER DUNNE

Fate. Destiny. A "sign." Whatever we call it,
there is a moment when we realize something
is meant to be. Friends constantly come to us
with requests for a certain kind of advice. Every
job we've had has somehow involved using a
particular skill. The kids in our neighborhood
are always showing up to watch us work in our
flower garden or woodshop.

It could be just a natural rhythm, a curious
little repetition in our life—or it could be more.
Finally, we think, "Maybe I should do something
about that" and turn it into a business idea, a
neighborhood group, a class, a book.

I will watch for the patterns in my life and answer
their call.

Holistic life

"*Living well and beautifully and justly are all one thing.*"

—⟶ SOCRATES

We tend to compartmentalize our lives: work, personal, friends, spiritual, financial, health, recreation. Some days, it seems as if they all compete with each other. It's best to let all our facets radiate from a core set of values.

Acts of justice and compassion can be personally enriching—and even fun. Enjoying an athletic activity can be a good way to share a relationship with others. Delighting in our work leads to a more playful attitude at home. Creating a sustainable lifestyle helps our bank accounts while it reduces stress and offers spiritual transformation. All the seemingly unrelated elements of life are actually closely intertwined, feeding and influencing each other in a constant spiral.

I celebrate and encourage the interdependence of all my pursuits and desires.

Real happiness

"Happiness comes more from loving than being loved; and often when our affection seems wounded it is only our vanity bleeding. To love, and to be hurt often, and to love again—this is the brave and happy life."

—J.E. BUCHROSE

Happiness is not found by protecting ourselves from events and relationships that might disappoint or grieve us. Hiding from risk doesn't keep a person happy and well. Just as our muscles need to be worked and exercised for our bodies to be healthy, our minds and emotions require the practice and stretching of risk to be whole, well, and happy.

Our souls seem made for the risks of relationship and growth; without those in our lives, a big part of who we are begins to die. Accepting the challenge of connection and the potential for hurt, we flourish and experience moments of real happiness.

I will take the risk of connecting with others.

Connected through kindness

"*Kindness is the golden chain by which society is bound together.*"

—JOHANN WOLFGANG VON GOETHE

In the midst of a busy day, we are surprised when someone steps aside and lets us go first, stoops to pick up an item we dropped, or holds the elevator door. Maybe a friend stops by with an unexpected cup of our favorite coffee. The moment sweetens our day, standing out against the backdrop of routine.

Kindness is a surprise that heightens our awareness. We are alert to the gift we receive—and then feel joyfully obligated to pass it along. Kindness reminds us that we are not alone.

I am grateful for all the kindness I received today. I will pass that kindness forward.

Relationships matter most

"Man is a knot, a web, a mesh into which relationships are tied. Only those relationships matter."

— ANTOINE DE SAINT-EXUPÉRY

We often search for our identity alone. That search may be a private labor, but the definition and function of identity comes through our relationships with others.

Who we are comes to life when we stand in contrast, in tension, or in harmony with those around us. Our movement and interaction with other people creates the story that matters. Individually, we are backdrops for the experiences that play out when two or more of us converse or conflict.

My great range of relationships, from the most casual acquaintance to the closest friend, matter deeply. Together, we create the experience of life. I am glad I am not alone.

Trust

> "*He who does not trust enough, will not be trusted.*"
>
> —☽ LAO TZU

Trust is a precious gift; it needs to be earned and maintained. That doesn't mean we must be suspicious of others until they've earned our trust. If we distrust people, we'll likely get just what we expect. If we look for the negative, we will find it.

It is an art to regard people with an open, although perhaps ambivalent, mind. We tend to judge a person immediately, but it takes time to see the qualities of another's character. When we are open to the idea that most people are trust-worthy, we may discover something surprising: They are.

I am open to trusting people. I will look for those who display solid character qualities rather than focusing on those who have disappointed me.

Invisible strands

"Faith is the centerpiece of a connected life. It allows us to live by the grace of invisible strands. It is a belief in a wisdom superior to our own. Faith becomes a teacher in the absence of fact."

—◌ TERRY TEMPEST WILLIAMS

When life seems uncertain, we try to regain a sense that all is well and our needs will be met. Yet, most character development occurs when we are living through a time when we are decidedly not in control. It might be a difficult trial or sickness, or a season of intense creativity and action.

Somehow, in the midst of what appears chaotic, we see an orchestration not of our own hand. Our connection to others and the world around us becomes clearer as helpful "chance" happenings occur.

I am grateful for the invisible strands guiding and connecting my life experience. There is a greater wisdom orchestrating my life.

Faith and reason

> *Faith is the art of holding on to things your reason has once accepted, in spite of your changing moods.*
>
> —C.S. LEWIS

Faith and reason are not necessarily at odds. As multiple facets of who we are, they often work to support each other. Faith may expand the boundaries of reason when it spurs us to try something new or brings hope to a disheartening moment. Reason sees the tangible fruit of faith and accepts that new reality as sound.

When reality is tested and our emotions waver, faith steps in to remind us that our belief is reasonable and worth retaining. Faith and reason become an inseparable team.

I realize I need both faith and reason in all growth and challenge.

No longer intimidated

"No one can make you feel inferior without your consent."

—⸻ ELEANOR ROOSEVELT

Confidence bubbles up from within. Nothing anyone says or does can shake a truly confident core. When we feel inferior or intimidated, it is usually because we have put our sense of confidence in someone else's hands. Their judgments about our work or who we are suddenly have great sway over our own confidence. Longing for approval, we seek it from someone else, forgetting that it was in our power all along.

I take back my confidence. I will not let another person's opinions shake my core sense of worth.

Speak your thoughts

"I have come to believe over and over again that what is most important to me must be spoken, made verbal and shared, even at the risk of having it bruised or misunderstood."

—⌐ AUDRE LORDE

It is vital to put words to our thoughts. When we have an important decision to make, we often say "I need to talk this through," or "I need a sounding board." Our beliefs and values come to life and become more tangible when we speak them or write them down in hope of sharing them.

When we keep our thoughts inside, it's almost like we're hiding. So, we take the risk and speak. Afterwards, not only does the other person know more about us, we know more about ourselves.

I choose to speak my thoughts on what matters to me. It might be hard to find the right words, and the other person might not understand, but it is worth the effort to share who I really am.

Laugh at yourself

"You grow up the day you have your first real laugh at yourself."

—⊖ ETHEL BARRYMORE

So much tension in life comes from taking ourselves a bit too seriously. We learn to laugh at ourselves when we realize that the personal image, status, and the impression we project are all superficial.

There is nothing wrong with trying to appear collected and flawless, but we are human and we do make mistakes. It's a relief to recognize how funny those mistakes are. In our own laughter, we find the freedom to grow.

I remember recent times when I've tripped over my own feet, figuratively or literally. I can give myself a break and smile and laugh about it now.

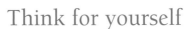
Think for yourself

"Be yourself and think for yourself; and while your conclusions may not be infallible, they will be nearer right than the conclusions forced upon you."

—☙ ELBERT HUBBARD

If we're going to make a mistake, why not make it boldly? We grow the most when we learn for ourselves. The hallmark of maturity isn't necessarily that we live and choose perfectly 100 percent of the time. We need to take a risk, come to a conclusion and test it to develop understanding and wisdom. Maturity means having a teachable spirit, a willingness to learn from mistakes and adjust our conclusions where needed.

It's okay for me to make mistakes as I learn about something new. It's all part of the process of learning even more.

Taking shape

"I would rather think of life as a good book. The further you get into it, the more it begins to come together and make sense."

— RABBI HAROLD KUSHNER

Every day is full of questions. It's only as days, weeks, and months go by that we're able to look back and see a pattern. Then, there is an intelligence to it all.

Years go by, and our character develops. We make choices as we set and achieve our goals. Life brings us unexpected joys and sorrows that become integral to our development. Like a grand patchwork quilt, none of the individual moments makes sense or seems to have much value by itself. Woven together, a work of art takes shape.

Sometimes I'm not sure why I had to go through a certain chapter in my life. I trust that those moments will make more sense as I move forward. Meanwhile, I am thankful for the sense of adventure and mystery.

Revealing our flaws

"It's just like magic. When you live by yourself, all your annoying habits are gone!"

—◌ MERRILL MARKOE

That would be the quick way to fix our character flaws! It's true, our flaws come to light primarily in the context of our relationship with others, but it doesn't justify isolating ourselves.

It may seem more comfortable at first to retreat, but, ultimately, our loved ones help reveal our strengths. Even when we annoy each other, we are learning powerful lessons about how to relate to others—who may be very different from ourselves—and how to grow through conflict.

I will take the risk of drawing closer to people I love. I am thankful for the way we sharpen each other's strengths, and I can laugh at how we can get on each other's nerves at times.

Learning from mistakes

"It is natural to make mistakes; it is terribly wrong to willfully keep making mistakes."

— St. Augustine

Learning requires trial and error. We need to give ourselves permission to mess up—and we must learn from those mistakes. Pride or stubbornness might keep us trying the same unwise action. We make much more progress—and our loved ones sure appreciate it—when we dust off after a fall, admit our error, and then try a smarter approach.

It's okay and even healthy for me to make mistakes. But, I want to look for ways to learn from those mistakes.

A promise kept

"A promise is a cloud; fulfillment is rain."

—$\backsim$ ARABIAN PROVERB

When someone makes us a promise, we can only listen in hope. We want to believe promises, but sometimes past disappointments get in the way. Will he really come through? Will she really do what she said she would?

Once we see the promise honored, it is not only the fulfillment that delights us. We also delight in our strengthened trust with the one who made the promise. Every time a promise is kept, integrity grows and the relationship deepens.

Promises mean a lot, but only a fulfilled promise can strengthen my relationships. I will keep my promises and show gratitude to those who honor their promises to me.

Work and family life

"*In work, do what you enjoy. In family life, be completely present.*"

—◦ LAO TZU

Drudgery sets in when we're working at a job we do not like, but it's a wonderful feeling to be working at an activity we enjoy. A balanced life requires that we have a rich life outside of our work life, no matter how much we love our job.

When we go home to family—whether we have a spouse and children of our own or are visiting relatives or family-like friends—we need to choose to be present with them. We are no longer in work mode. It's time for relationship, play, empathy, and care.

I want to live a life well balanced between satisfying work and dynamic family life. I will guide my attention and focus to be fully present wherever I am at the moment.

Escaping dept

"Debt is a trap which man sets and baits himself, and then deliberately gets into."

— JOSH BILLINGS

Borrowing is a quick way to get what we want sooner than if we had saved for it. But, with some purchases, the debt stays with us long after what we bought has been used up or lost its value. We're left with a memory—and an interest rate. We know better, but like any bad habit, amassing debt can be a hard cycle to break.

We need to admit that we're baiting and trapping ourselves. Then, it's time to start practicing the old art of living within our means and saving for what we want. Those are the basic building blocks for getting out of the trap of debt. It's such a pleasure that first time we make a large purchase with cash instead of a credit card.

The next time I consider going into debt to make a purchase, I will take time to weigh the cost and look for an alternative to buying on credit.

Keep going

"I take a simple view of living. It is, keep your eyes open and get on with it."

—SIR LAURENCE OLIVIER

There are times when all we can do is stay our present course. We need to be alert to alternatives and obstacles that may show up, but the path we've chosen is the best possible option for now. Let's not waste time fussing over the details; we'll pick up our pack and keep going.

There's a time and place for scrutinizing my routine and lifestyle. There are also times when it's best to simply move forward.

Life's purpose

> *"I finally figured out the only reason to be alive is to enjoy it."*
>
> — RITA MAE BROWN

Spending pleasant time with friends and family, discovering work that suits us well, playing outdoors, reading a good book—there are hundreds of daily moments when we touch on our reason for living. It's not lofty grand purpose; it is genuine delight and gratitude for the moment we're in. It is experiencing each moment with as much joy as possible.

Perhaps my life isn't so complicated. What's important is to live it well and joyfully. I can do that right now.

Responsive or reactive?

"I must govern the clock, not be governed by it."

—⌒ GOLDA MEIR

It is common to be reactive when we feel pressed for time. We feel defensive and let emergencies and interruptions command our day. Our main motivations are fear and worry.

When we are responsive instead of reactive, we act from a place of personal security. We know what we want out of our time each day. We are aware and honest about the time needed for certain tasks, and we set a reasonable schedule. When a surprise comes, we decide first if it is something we *must* do, and then how we will fit it into our day. No amount of false urgency shakes us from giving the matter, and ourselves, appropriate time.

I can turn off the chatter of stress and hurry in my mind. I will pause, collect myself, and get back in command.

Harsh truth

" Truth is a rough, honest, helter-skelter terrier, that none like to see brought into their drawing rooms. "

—Ⓢ OUIDA

Sometimes the truth hurts. We don't want to face it when it cuts to the heart of a vulnerable issue or reveals plainly that we need to change ourselves or our plans. Is it better to keep our head in the sand? If there is a problem with one of our ideas or plans, isn't it better to hear it? When we listen to the truth, messy and unpleasant as it may be, we can begin to change for the better.

Even though it's uncomfortable, I will listen to the truth. It may seem damaging to something I hold dear, but I would rather have that than live an illusion.

When friendship begins

" We cannot tell the precise moment when friendship is formed. As in filling a vessel drop by drop, there is at last a drop which makes it run over. So in a series of kindnesses there is, at last, one which makes the heart run over. "

—⚬ JAMES BOSWELL

We never know when one of our kind gestures to someone in our circle of acquaintances will overflow into friendship. All we know is that, one day, when we want to talk or when we want to share a leisure activity, we think of calling someone we never thought about calling before. Or, perhaps they contact us. The slightest turn is made; we have—and we are—a new friend.

I can't remember when all of my friendships began, but I am so glad I reached out and continued to do so until we became the friends we are today.

The power of a kind word

"Kind words can be short and easy to speak, but their echoes are truly endless."

—◌ MOTHER TERESA

We smile at a store clerk who seems a little tired and encourage him to hang in there: "You're doing a great job." Sometimes when we say things like that, it falls on deaf ears. The other person is simply too busy to hear it. Once in a while, though, small, kind gestures seem to lift a big burden from others' shoulders. Their eyes brighten, their mouths soften into grins. We know our simple but honest comment may have been a day-brightener. That knowledge is its own reward.

I will look for opportunities to speak encouraging words to people in my life. My dear friends and total strangers are all in need of hearing they are precious and that I appreciate them.

Many interests, many friends

> *"I cannot concentrate all my friendship on any single one of my friends because no one is complete enough in himself."*
>
> — ANAÏS NIN

Each one of us is an unusual mix of interests, preferences, ideas, and passions. No single person is likely to enjoy all our facets. It can cause tension when we expect a dear friend to take up one of our interests just because we want a partner.

It's far more gracious to satisfy our need for social connection by meeting and making friends with a wide range of people. One person goes swimming with us. Another likes to discuss spirituality. Another enjoys our hobby of restoring old cars. There are many good pals who can meet us wherever we're at, whatever we're doing.

My best friend might not enjoy everything that I do. That's okay. I will make a few new friends who like some of the interests that I've been enjoying lately.

Prayer of gratitude

"If the only prayer you say in your whole life is 'Thank you,' that would suffice."

— MEISTER ECKHART

Our prayers do not need to be long, loud, or eloquent to be powerful. In fact, the most meaningful prayers are not *for* anything. They are a simple awareness of all we already have. We quiet the fussy thoughts about the day and cease yearning for answers. Resting into a focused state of gratitude is the most important prayer we can learn.

Thank you—for this day, for this moment, for all the good in my life right now.

Balanced life

"A day's work is a day's work, neither more nor less, and the man who does it needs a day's sustenance, a night's repose and due leisure, whether he be painter or ploughman."

—⌒ GEORGE BERNARD SHAW

Sometimes we work so long, our fatigue makes us vulnerable to stress-related illnesses. Then we discover the activities that seemed to be luxuries—like exercise at the gym, a daily walk, or a good night's sleep—were actually deep needs.

No matter who we are or what we do for a living, just as our bodies require balanced diets, our souls have their own needs for balance and moderation. Eat, sleep, work, and play. In rotating fashion, these activities sustain and inspire harmony.

It's pleasant to lead a balanced life with time for meeting all my soul's needs. I will protect the time I set aside for sustenance, rest, and leisure.

Self-absorbed

"*A man wrapped up in himself makes a very small bundle.*"

—⌐ BENJAMIN FRANKLIN

It can be hard to carry on a conversation with people who are completely absorbed in their own affairs. Whether they are irritated, excited, or lamenting, they have blinders on toward anyone else's concerns. It doesn't feel like they're talking with us so much as talking *at* us. It's exhausting, and annoying, to be on the receiving end.

We can remember how that feels and be careful not to make the same mistake ourselves. Even when our own lives take up most of our inner monologue, we can be considerate to others, welcoming their input and asking what's on their mind.

My conversations and relationships are more fun when everyone gets to have a say. I'll be careful not to take over the airwaves.

Moving beyond optimism

"Optimism, unaccompanied by personal effort, is merely a state of mind and not fruitful."

— ✦ EDWARD L. CURTIS

Positive thinking is a powerful force to fuel change. But, optimism alone is just wood stacked in the woodpile. We have to bring it inside, build a fire, and tend it. Otherwise, it remains no more than dry wood. Like the wood, optimism has a shelf life. Left unused, it seems to rot. We must keep it moving, bringing in fresh fuel and using it up.

I will attach specific, achievable plans to my optimistic attitude. My optimism will be the fuel that gets things started.

The right time for decisions

> *"Form a habit of making decisions when your spirit is fresh . . . to let dark moods lead is like choosing cowards to command armies."*
> — CHARLES HORTON COOLEY

Unfortunately, when that dark mood sets in, we are prone to push the panic button and come to a snap decision. Those panicky decisions tend to make more trouble—which only further darkens our mood.

We can train ourselves to do it differently. With gentle self-talk, we remind ourselves that we don't make large decisions when we're tired, blue, or hungry. It can wait until we are rested, centered, and well fed. Good decisions produce better results.

I won't make serious decisions when I'm spent. I'll wait until I can give the matter the clear thought that it deserves.

Strong people get help

"The healthy, the strong individual, is the one who asks for help when he needs it. Whether he has an abscess on his knee or in his soul."

—✑ RONA BARRETT

Asking for help is not a sign of weakness; it's a hallmark of maturity. Being able to recognize that we need help, and finding the right person to help us, takes courage and insight. Too often, we try to go it alone, pushing ourselves until we're in a complete mess. We can avoid a lot of suffering if we face the fact that we need help and speak up sooner.

Whether I need physical assistance or just advice, I won't wait until it's an emergency to get help. I'll acknowledge my need early on and let someone know I have a problem. There are people in my life who care deeply for me and would be more than happy to help.

Forgiveness frees us

"Forgiveness is the key to action and freedom."
— HANNAH ARENDT

We forgive and discover we have not given in. We have not lost. On the contrary, we can finally move and stretch again. The bitterness was only eating at us; it had done nothing to affect the one who offended us. Having forgiven the wrong, we no longer have to focus on it and ruminate about it. It no longer has to be a part of our everyday life. We can get back to living.

I am thankful for the power of forgiveness.

Sleep without burdens

> " *To carry care to bed is to sleep with a pack on your back.* "
>
> —◌ THOMAS C. HALIBURTON

What concerns are we mulling over right now? Do they keep us awake or make our sleep fitful? We wouldn't expect anyone to sleep well wearing a backpack. Like a hiker who releases the clasps on a heavy pack and breathes a satisfied sigh of relief to be free of the burden, we can set our thoughts aside now.

I've done well carrying my pack of concerns and decisions today. Now, I can sit by the campfire in my mind, slip out of this pack, and listen to my own breathing as I fall asleep.

Smile, and feel better

"Get out of bed forcing a smile. You may not smile because you are cheerful; but if you will force yourself to smile you'll be cheerful because you smile. Repeated experiments prove that when man assumes the facial expression of a given mental mood, any given mood, then that mental mood itself will follow."

— KENNETH GOODE

We've heard it works; we've even experienced it. Look bright and cheerful and it starts to lift our energy up. It's not about faking it or being superficial. The change is deep and profound. Are mornings tough? Why not try an experimental smile? It can't hurt. Smiles are contagious. At the very least, we might cheer someone up as we go through our morning routine.

I'll write myself a note reminding me to smile tomorrow morning. It's worth trying.

Memory recalls moments

*"We do not remember days, we
remember moments."*

—◌ CESARE PAVESE

Remember that time when we . . . When we reminisce, we begin with a reference to a specific
moment. Memory is peculiar that way. It's amazing the amount of detail we can remember about
a certain intriguing, hilarious, or frightening
moment. The rest of the day during which that
moment occurred may be completely forgotten.
Our lives become a quilt of significant moments,
while the rest gently fade.

Moments are what matter. I am thankful for all the
joyful moments I remember. I gently carry the difficult ones. I create, day-by-day, new moments to
remember tomorrow.

Friendship in adversity

"Adversity not only draws people together, but brings forth that beautiful inward friendship."

—⟶ SØREN KIERKEGAARD

Small emergencies and big crises alike have a way of bringing out the best in us. Whether it's a neighborhood rallying around one of its own who is fighting cancer, or a nation coming together to help a region devastated by natural disaster, there are inspiring stories of how resourceful and cooperative we can be.

Fighting for a common ideal, we bond together and communicate in greater depth. We find ourselves working alongside someone we wouldn't normally talk to and discover a new friend. Redemption and transformation can come about in the midst of adversity.

I don't wish a hard time on anyone, but I am grateful for the unique redemption that only occurs during adversity.

Empty flattery

"Flatterers look like friends, as wolves like dogs."
— George Chapman

Compliments feel fantastic. We like to be around people who give us positive feedback. But our antennae perk up when someone seems to speak too many good things about us. Flattery makes us skeptical. Do they really admire us, or are they trying to get something? It's wise to be cautious when we interact with flatterers. Say a simple "thank you," but don't become dependent on sugary words. In the end, the highest compliments come from those who do not give them often.

I like hearing that I have done well and look sharp, but I can tell when compliments have evolved into flattery. I will be cautious with someone who is prone to flattery; there may be strings attached.

True contentment

"Good friends, good books, and a sleepy conscience: This is the ideal life."

—☙ MARK TWAIN

Sometimes, when we take a retreat alone or with loved ones, we find ourselves taking deep pleasure in the smallest moments. We sit by the fire reading a good book or chatting with a dear friend and we think, "This is living!" How simple it is. We can take that sensibility home with us, setting the stage for a life of gentle rest and straightforward integrity.

I can create a life that puts meaningful things first. Anything beyond that is just extra—and I won't let those extras take over.

We number our days

"So teach us to number our days, that we may apply our hearts unto wisdom."

— Psalms 90:12

To "number our days" means to hold in our hearts a constant gentle awareness of how brief and precious our time is. That awareness isn't meant to make us feel fearful of days' end or overly worried about wasted time. It is meant to spark our commitment to continue to learn and lay hold of life. Our commitment to grow flows into a quest for wisdom, which ensures that we use our time here well.

My time here is short. That doesn't have to be a sad thought. It can inspire me to be mindful about how I spend my days.

Map a straight course

> *The man of fixed ingrained principles who has mapped out a straight course, and has the courage and self-control to adhere to it, does not find life complex. Complexities are all of our own making.*
>
> —◠ B.C. FORBES

There are times when life may be high-stress. We move, change jobs, struggle with an illness, start a new friendship, or end a relationship. Life's highs and lows can both cause stress. We can choose how complicated we make the situation. We can calmly evaluate, plot our course, and do it, or we can obsess over minute details and fuss about whether we have the bravery to carry out our plan. We can decide whether to see any situation in either simple or complicated ways.

I don't need to make things complicated. Whether it's a hard time or a happy one, I can navigate the waters in the straightest line possible.

Love heals

> " *Throughout history, 'tender loving care' has uniformly been recognized as a valuable element in healing.* "
>
> — DR. LARRY DOSSEY

People recover faster when they have loved ones actively encouraging them and expressing care. We are social creatures; our needs do not stop at the physical basics. We need relationships and positive feedback just as we need physical nourishment, shelter, and medical care.

Someone may recover poorly from a trauma simply because there is no one loving them through the crisis. Any time we speak loving words to someone who is hurting, or receive encouragement when we are sick, we are participating in a healing act.

I will express gratitude toward a few people who have cared for me during a hard time. I will watch for others in need of compassion and pass on the kindness.

Joy perpetuates itself

> *When I have been unhappy, I have heard an*
> *opera . . . and it seemed the shrieking of winds;*
> *when I am happy, a sparrow's chirp is delicious to*
> *me. But it is not the chirp that makes me happy,*
> *but I that make it sweet.*
>
> — JOHN RUSKIN

Just as depression colors even good things gray,
joy colors all things brighter. When we live
with an attitude of happiness and joy, it is self-
reinforcing. With a positive outlook, we see even
more reasons to be joyful. Even very simple
pleasures warm the joy-filled heart.

Happiness is an attitude I can choose each day. I
will make that choice and see how it brings me
even more reasons to be joyful.

One's own person

"Self-reliance is the only road to true freedom, and being one's own person is its ultimate reward."

—⌒ PATRICIA SAMPSON

We need other people. Self-reliance doesn't mean we're isolated or standoffish. It means that, when connecting with others, we do so as sufficient people. We don't tax another person or demand they meet our needs.

Becoming self-reliant is rewarding not only to our own level of self-confidence, but also to set the stage for healthier relationships. Whole and happy, we enjoy our own company and relate to others with greater depth and respect.

I want to become more self-reliant. It can make me more confident—and help me become a better friend to others.

Refill the lamp

"To keep a lamp burning, we have to keep putting oil in it."

—MOTHER TERESA

It is blessed to give, but we need to watch for the risk of burning out. Most spiritual traditions teach that giving is a circular flow. Ideally, we give out of recognition of our joyful abundance. Trouble typically starts when we give out of a sense of obligation or guilt. That's when we get that drained, spread-too-thin feeling.

Guilt tells us to give more, when what we may need to do—for our sake and everyone else's—is take a break. It is a spiritual and generous act to take time for doing nothing, for letting the well refill.

I will watch for the signs of burnout in myself and in my loved ones. I will make time to rest and refuel.

Unanswered questions

"*Live your questions now, and perhaps even without knowing it, you will live along some distant day into your answers.*"

—⌒ RAINER MARIA RILKE

We long for answers and more control when a situation seems uncertain. We want a quick fix for our own hurts, bad habits, and idiosyncrasies. Sometimes we miss the lessons we could be learning along the way as we live the question. Turning the question over and over, focusing on the irritation, we actually give it more power.

Perhaps we're trying too hard. When we let go of the question and go on living, we let ourselves focus on other things and be joyful again. Often, we then find where the answer was all along.

I can get tired of hearing about the importance of "the process," but I know it's true. I accept that I don't have all the answers I want; I can let myself live the questions.

Cultivate physical health

> ❝*Our bodies are our gardens—our wills are our gardeners.*❞
>
> —❧ WILLIAM SHAKESPEARE

Our time here in our bodies is precious. We tend the garden we've been given, but it is a choice each day to care for it or not. Just as a literal garden shows evidence of the attention it has received, our own bodies tell the story of the kind of care we give them—whether the barest minimum of nourishment and occasional movement, the most extravagant self-care and well-planned exercise, or anything in between.

I am happy to cultivate my physical self just as a gardener enjoys nurturing the plants in a garden. I can get a massage, cook a healthy meal, or start a yoga class to pay more attention to my body.

Know yourself, act accordingly

"Ninety percent of the world's woe comes from people not knowing themselves, their abilities, their frailties, and even their real virtues."

—◌ SYDNEY J. HARRIS

It's frustrating to try to be something we're not. It feels constricting when we're not in the right place, whether it's the wrong job or a lifestyle that's not healthy for our body or soul. We've all had the experience of interacting with someone who is living out of sync with their identity. The tension is constant; it might show in flashes of temper or constant low-grade blues.

How pleasant it is when we know ourselves well enough to build a life that resonates with who we are. Even greater is the experience of living and working with others who are making similar choices. The harmony and joy are palpable.

I take time to examine my own strengths, weaknesses, values, loves, and fears. I listen to myself and make choices appropriate to who I am.

Ask in love

66 *The simple heart that freely asks in love, obtains.* 99

—⌒ JOHN GREENLEAF WHITTIER

When a request is centered in love, it is much more likely to be fulfilled. Whether our wish is expressed toward the Divine or to someone close to us, when we come from a state of simple focus and love, we think more honestly about the nature of the request. How will our desire affect others? Do we really need this? Is it truly beneficial? The universe is ready to answer the longing of hearts that wish to leave the world a better place for themselves and others.

Before making requests in prayer or conversation, I will center my soul in love and focus my mind on simplicity.

Accolades

"He who seeks for applause only from without has all his happiness in another's keeping."

—ᴄᴏ OLIVER GOLDSMITH

It's nice to get positive feedback. We hope our loved ones let us know when we've done well, but our sense of worth needs to come from the affirmations we give ourselves. We become true adults when we realize we don't need applause in order to move forword. Free of the need for external approval, we can grow and stand solid in our own values and passions. Our sense of confidence is no longer dependent on others' opinions.

I am glad to hear compliments and accolades once in a while, but that is not the barometer for my own self-confidence.

Your own brainstorming

"You are the product of your own brainstorm."
— ROSEMARY KONNER STEINBAUM

Our thoughts are powerful. Focused thoughts lead to decisions which determine our life path. At one time or another, we have thought of a class we'd like to take, a dream job we'd like to research, a person we would like to get to know, a place we would like to visit, an old friend we would like to call.

Those seemingly random thoughts have led to life-changing choices. The lifestyle we created affected the development of our character, relationships, and attitudes. Who would have imagined a simple brainstorm could be so powerful?

I will take my brainstorms seriously, giving myself time to dream up new ideas. I will carefully choose the ones I will entertain further.

Change and growth

"*Change and growth take place when a person has risked himself and dares to become involved with experimenting with his own life.*"

—⟶ HERBERT OTTO

Life can turn stagnant. Sometimes we get the feeling that we are stuck in a rut. Healthy organisms grow naturally, and we are no different. We know something is off when it seems we're no longer expanding our treasure trove of understanding and experience.

It's time to play a little. Change may be scary, but it is necessary to find and consume the spiritual nourishment we've apparently been missing. We must experiment to discover what we need to begin growing again.

I will take a risk in order to bring healthy change and fresh energy into my life. I'm not sure what it will take, but I will experiment with a few options that come to my mind right now.

Life is messy

"*Maturity is achieved when a person accepts life as full of tension.*"

—JOSHUA LOTH LIEBMAN

Most sources of stress come from fears and concerns over factors we cannot control. When there is tension in our lives, our initial reaction is to want to fix it, to make it better. But life is messy. The more we risk and love, the more we grow—and the more we make ourselves vulnerable to further conflict, obstacles, and tension.

At the heart of serenity and maturity is a willingness to release our need to control or remove all sources of tension. With that, we free ourselves to grow even more.

I am so glad it's not my responsibility to fix every problem and tension in my life! I will let go of the small stuff, so I can free myself to live and grow.

Use it or lose it

*"Good for the body is the work of the body, good
for the soul the work of the soul, and good for
either the work of the other."*

—⟶ HENRY DAVID THOREAU

Just as our muscles benefit from work and
stretching, our souls benefit from challenge. The
soul delights in taking on relational development, spiritual practice, and fresh thoughts.

Soul and body are interdependent. We may
remember a time when a health issue affected
our souls; we felt disappointed when our physical life was limited. Likewise, the soul's ups and
downs may affect our choices about how we
care for our bodies.

I will care for both my body and my soul to create
an upward spiral of health.

Actions are louder

"Well done is better than well said."

—⎯ BENJAMIN FRANKLIN

We respect a person whose actions line up with their words. Even more impressive are those who live their values and let their choices speak for themselves. It's easy to talk about how we think things ought to be, harder to develop and then carry out a plan for change.

I admire people who walk their talk. I can be that person, too. The next time I feel like complaining, I'll think about a small way to change the situation—and then do it.

Our highest business

"We are involved in a life that passes understanding; our highest business is our daily life."

—JOHN CAGE

Life can feel a little mundane at times, but think for a moment of the miracles of our daily life. Think of the processes going on in our bodies without our awareness, the technologies we take for granted, and the intricacies of the routine we've created. Think about how well it all flows. It may be daily life because it has become familiar to us, but each day we live many wonders.

I am grateful for my daily life; it is an honor to live it. My day-to-day routine holds many mysteries, even though it has become ordinary and comfortable to me.

Like packing a suitcase

" The real secret of how to use time is to pack it as you would a portmanteau, filling up the small spaces with small things. "

—❧ SIR HENRY HADDOW

We've all packed a bag for an outing or a lengthy trip. We know we want to be prepared for several planned activities and some contingencies, too. Having stacked all the most important items inside, we then start tucking little things into the remaining nooks and crannies. It's amazing how much we can fit in there!

Similarly, with time, it's important that we start by "packing" the most important and time-consuming things. All the miscellaneous little tasks will fit neatly between the big plans. Whether packing a suitcase or scheduling a day, if the small stuff goes in first, it can crowd out the big items. If we reverse the order, everything tends to fit neatly, just like a puzzle.

I will tuck my minor tasks efficiently into the natural gaps between more important commitments.

The best persuasion

"The most effective persuasion is a life well lived."

— ANNA BJÖRKLUND

We can talk at length about a cause or belief we hold dear, but it's rare that words alone persuade anyone. At some point, we need to quietly let our actions speak for themselves. Others are inspired to learn more about our beliefs and values when they see us effecting change through our daily life, not simply our words.

I don't always need to use words to get my point across. Sometimes all I have to do is let my life speak for itself.

Time versus money

"Dollars cannot buy yesterday."
— ADMIRAL HAROLD R. STARK

In eulogies, people are rarely lauded for how much money they made. They almost always are remembered for how they spent their time. When all is said and done, schedules and finances are important, but our time is more valuable. Time is the most important investment we can make in our relationships. Wasted money may be recovered eventually; lost time is gone forever.

When I'm weighing decisions that involve both time and money, I will remember that time is priceless.

Change begins in the body

"Movement is a medicine for creating change in a person's physical, emotional, and mental states."

—⟶ CAROL WELCH

Our body, feelings, and thoughts are all connected. When we are feeling tense, our bodies show it.

Releasing our muscle tension with a relaxing exercise or meditation can ease our mind and soothe our emotions. If we fail to solve a certain problem with pen and paper, sometimes the best thing we can do is go for a walk. When we feel closed off to people, we tend to look down. If we deliberately choose to look up and drop our shoulders, we suddenly feel at ease and others see us as more approachable.

I wonder if my posture and movement may be reinforcing a difficult issue in my life. I will look for ways to change my physical stance and see if that helps my thoughts and emotions.

One day at a time

"Home wasn't built in a day."

—⌒ JANE ACE

The dust on the television screen is so thick,
we're amazed our family members can even
see the programs they watch. The grass in the
backyard is so tall, rabbits can hide in it. And our
inbox at work is so full it is literally tipping over.

We can be easily overwhelmed by endless
housekeeping and professional workloads. We
might even have trouble sleeping, wondering
how we will ever catch up on our responsibili-
ties. But if we tackle one simple task each time
we walk into a room, we can slowly make a
dent in the work. More important, we'll be
able to sleep well at night, knowing this steady
approach will also help us accomplish whatever
tomorrow brings.

Instead of racing to finish tasks, I'll work calmly
and steadily until each job is done.

Importance of routine

"*If you do the same thing every day at the same time for the same length of time, you'll save yourself from many a sink. Routine is a condition of survival.*"

—⌁ FLANNERY O'CONNOR

Inviting change doesn't mean abandoning all old routines. By pursuing new goals every day without fail for at least two weeks, we develop newly ingrained habits that color and influence our days.

I need some routine in my life. Not only do I need to meet my most basic needs, I also want to include a few reflective activities that lift my spirits and keep me inspired.

Sentimentality

"What was hard to bear is sweet to remember."

— PORTUGUESE PROVERB

A tough time can become memorialized in our minds. In hindsight, we see more clearly the valuable aspects of what was difficult at the time. We had no money for dining out, but the simple recipes we relied on are our comfort foods today. The job was stressful, but we've never since worked with such a positive group of people. The house was always a mess, but how we miss the energy of the kids when they were young.

Even as we appreciate the beauty of the past, we can be more mindful about noticing the beauty in our lives today.

When I remember a particularly hard time in my life, I treasure some of the moments I experienced. As I look at my current challenges, I will try to recognize the precious aspects of my life right now.

Fear and caution

"The defense force inside of us wants us to be cautious, to stay away from anything as intense as a new kind of action. Its job is to protect us, and it categorically avoids anything resembling danger. But it's often wrong."

—— BARBARA SHER

Public speaking. Heights. Conflict with a loved one. Many things can trigger our fear response. Our heart rate increases, palms get sweaty, mouth turns dry, and we want to escape the situation.

It's impossible to avoid everything that scares us. Fears can hold us back if we let them. We need to keep our mind engaged and our spirit courageous. The only cure for an irrational fear is to boldly face it and carry on with our original plan.

Sometimes fear is helpful, but often it limits me. I will stay alert, not only to real threats, but also to "threats" that are blown out of proportion by the panic of fear. I can face my fear and talk myself through it.

Thrifty or stingy

> *"So often we rob tomorrow's memories by today's economies."*
>
> —⤷ JOHN MASON BROWN

Whether we are miserly with our time or with our finances, we can make choices that we live to regret. In the name of efficiency and thriftiness, sometimes we go overboard. Instead of thinking of a more economical option for the family vacation, we say "no" to leisure altogether. The kids grow up remembering only our sullen mood.

There are limits, and we need to be realistic. We also need to make life's little joys a priority. A good time doesn't have to break the bank or destroy our schedule.

Once in a while, I am overly protective about my time or money. I can loosen up a little and make it a priority to create some positive memories for the future.

Planting seeds

"Judge each day not by its harvest, but by the seeds you plant."

—⌐ ANONYMOUS

We reap what we've sown over time. The harvests are often momentary, though—when we achieve a big dream, when someone shows they've learned what we taught them, when we reach a milestone in life. Those moments require days of ordinary life leading up to them, days when we are diligently planting seeds. As we look at the deeds of today, we can pause to note some of the seeds we've planted and hope good things for their eventual harvest.

I may not have made any earth-shattering progress today, but I did plant some important seeds. That is just as important—if not more so.

Do what you love

> "*The road to happiness lies in two simple principles: Find what interests you and that you can do well, and put your whole soul into it—every bit of energy and ambition and natural ability that you have.*"
>
> —JOHN D. ROCKEFELLER III

The best possible work situation is to spend our days doing what we love. Many of us are not quite sure what that is. We have to figure out what interests us, and that takes experimenting, practice, and learning on our own time. Once we find it, we are likely to turn it into some sort of daily work. Passionate about the task and showing that we're good at it, we will stand out as business owners, employees, or homemakers. Our enthusiasm naturally draws the favor of those we serve.

I will look for ways to bring more of my interests into my daily work life. Meanwhile, I am grateful for the parts of my work that are a great match for my passion and skills.

Wings

"Be like the bird that, passing on her flight
awhile on boughs too slight, feels them give way
beneath her, and yet sings, knowing that she
hath wings."

—⌐♭ VICTOR HUGO

As we learn and expand our talents and abilities,
we become more confident. Once confident,
we no longer fret so much if something in life
feels insecure or uncertain. We know we can
deal with situations that come up. We've landed
on our feet in the past when things got dicey;
we will again. Comfortable in our ability to face
what comes, our attitude and bearing are more
collected and joyful.

I will delight in my own abilities and appreciate my
self-confidence. I will hold my head high, knowing
that I can handle whatever tomorrow brings.

Forgive and remember

❝*The stupid neither forgive nor forget; the naïve forgive and forget; the wise forgive, but do not forget.*❞

—⌒ THOMAS SZASZ

"Forgive and forget," the saying goes. Forgive and gently remember may be more realistic. By forgiving, we relinquish our desire to get back at others. We release them from their offenses, and release ourselves from grudge-keeping and bitterness.

We do not forget, though. It takes time to rebuild trust. We have learned from what happened. Perhaps we will adjust the relationship a bit to avoid a repeat scenario. It is good to remember, but best if we don't grasp the memory so tightly.

I can forgive, even though I do not forget. I release the other person, but I am wise about adjusting my course as a result of what happened.

Remembering your neighbor

"A man is called selfish not for pursuing his own
good, but for neglecting his neighbor's."

—⟋ RICHARD WHATELY

We should not feel guilty for taking care of ourselves. We lapse into selfishness when we are no
longer moved by the needs of others. There are
opportunities every day to help and encourage
our neighbors, whether that means a member of
our nearby community or one far away.

Thinking of and caring for others does not
have to involve large sums of money or mas-
sive change. A smile and a kind word to a gas
station clerk can make a world of difference. As
soon as we make even a gesture that small, we
shatter selfishness by remembering the welfare
of others.

I will break through selfishness by opening my eyes
to the needs of others. Then I will commit daily to
simple actions that lessen the load for them.

Precious time

> **"***AIDS presents me with a choice: the choice either to be a hopeless victim and die of AIDS, or to make my life right now what it always ought to have been.***"**
>
> ——⌇ GRAHAM, A PERSON WITH AIDS

Most of us, when we are healthy, don't think about the brevity of our time here. We take many things for granted and get caught up in routine and petty problems.

Then illness strikes, and we are suddenly aware that our time is short. Once we break through the shock and grief and come into acceptance, we set about to do everything that we always wanted. In short, we create a meaningful life. We don't have to wait for illness to create that urgency. Together, with our loved ones, we can create that kind of life now.

My life is precious. My loved ones are dear to me. I will treasure each day and make it meaningful.

Sudden clarity

"One's mind has a way of making itself up in the background, and it suddenly becomes clear what one means to do."

— ARTHUR CHRISTOPHER BENSON

We wrestle with a choice for weeks. Should we finish our education? We weigh the pros and cons, we research. Something still doesn't feel right. We set a deadline and talk to someone we respect. Then, suddenly, in the midst of that conversation, we realize we don't want to go back to school at all right now. Come to think of it, we have some opportunities at work that might provide the same education.

Our instinct was telling us something all along. It's interesting how often that happens. Laboring over a choice, we use all our standard decision-making tools, only to discover a wild card that changes everything. "That makes perfect sense," we say. "Why didn't I think of that sooner?"

I won't get too anxious about my decisions; I'll know what I need to do when the time comes.

Family skeleton

"If you cannot get rid of the family skeleton, you may as well make it dance."

—⌒ GEORGE BERNARD SHAW

We all have a mixed bag of happy and sad memories in our family histories. There may be devastating events and traits that no one wants to talk about. Sometimes families hide the truth instead of healing. It feels like a broken bone that was never set correctly and so mended off-kilter. In the end, hiding the truth doesn't help anyone.

What does it mean to make the ugly truth dance? It might mean using humor. It might mean finding creative healing ways to tell the truth in our own lives, even if the rest of the family isn't eager to do so. As we tell the truth in our little corner of the family, we feel freer.

I can find ways to acknowledge my family skeletons. I can be honest about them in creative ways. I can even do it in a way that brings joy and freedom to others.

Good manners

> "*Manners are a sensitive awareness of the feelings of others. If you have that awareness, you have good manners, no matter what fork you use.*"
>
> —⌐ EMILY POST

Manners are so much more than following a set of cultural norms. Norms vary from culture to culture—even from family to family. It's difficult to pick up on all the nuances of manners outside our own circle, but, if we're aware of those around us, we observe what they are doing and ask questions if we're not sure about something. Others notice this sensitivity on our part. They'll be quick to give us grace for a little faux pas and gently let us know if we've committed a cultural blunder.

I don't always know the details of social etiquette, but my awareness of others is far more important than carrying out a list of rules on how to dine properly. My connection with and respect for other people is what really matters.

It's all in your attitude

"Blame yourself if you have no branches of leaves; don't accuse the sun of partiality."

— CHINESE PROVERB

We look at someone else's life and wonder why it seems to be richer and more fruitful than our own. We try to tell ourselves we've been dealt a bad hand. When we're honest, though, we notice that most others have lived through hard times, too.

Everyone receives a mix of positive and negative experiences and resources, but our attitude and approach to these may be different. When we recognize all the good energy entering our lives—just like sunlight—we can do the work that transforms dirt and a few seeds into real nourishment.

I can lament my difficulties, or I can turn them into fuel. I choose to grow and yield fruit, using all the raw material in my life right now.

A perfect friend?

"We shall never have friends if we expect to find them without fault."

—⌒ THOMAS FULLER

Do we ever rule out friendship with someone because of some personal flaw we've seen in them? It is good to be careful about the character of those we choose for close friendship, but sometimes we are a little too quick with our judgments. We may miss out on a friendship that could bring fresh perspective into our lives. If we are impossible to please, we may find ourselves enjoying our high standards alone.

When I'm making new friends, I can balance my desire for certain character traits and qualities with a gracious understanding that people are not perfect.

Creating ourselves

"Trust yourself. Create the kind of self that you will be happy to live with all your life. Make the most of yourself by fanning the tiny, inner sparks of possibility into flames of achievement."

—GOLDA MEIR

We will live with ourselves for the rest of our lives. We get to decide what kind of people we will be. We must make sure we are becoming the kind of company we would like to keep!

Looking at ourselves and evaluating who we are in light of who we would like to be can be daunting. We wonder, "Will I ever really get there?" We will; we can trust ourselves to continue to grow and mature in wisdom. All we need to do is fan into flame the good and beautiful sparks we already carry within us.

I have a picture in my mind of who I would like to be in five to ten years. I know that vision will become reality as I start now, in small ways, to turn into that person.

The energy of spring

"Everything holds its breath except spring. She bursts through as strong as ever."

—B.M. BOWER

Every year the energy and movement of spring takes us by surprise. After the browns and grays of late winter, the vivid greens and bright colors of flowers break through the mud and cold. As days grow longer, we have more energy, too. The sun brightens dispositions and boosts our creativity and optimism.

Spring reminds us that, even in our high-tech age, the cycles of nature affect us deeply. We can take advantage of the renewed enthusiasm of this season.

I will take a walk in the spring sunshine, as soon as the weather allows it, and I'll listen for fresh ideas germinating in my mind.

Your own barometer

"When one is pretending, the entire body revolts."

—◌ ANAÏS NIN

From muscle knots in our shoulders to literally getting ill, great tension forms in the body when we begin to pretend or hide. The body prefers genuine living. We aren't wired to live lies or to try to be anyone but ourselves. If we try to hide our true desires, opinions, passions, interests, and memories, the body takes issue with the charade.

I will listen to any tension in my body right now. From where might it be coming? What area in my life might be creating stress and pushing me out of integrity?

Facing our problems

> "*Not everything that is faced can be changed, but nothing can be changed until it is faced.*"
>
> —JAMES BALDWIN

We have little or no power to change some problems in our lives. An injury or illness leaves us with physical limitations, a dear friend moves away, a shift at our company limits our career advancement. It's tempting to become bitter, but facing the problem is far healthier.

When we face the problem, we may find there are some parts of it we can change. Time and therapy help our injury or illness, a phone call with a friend results in scheduling a fun reunion, an honest chat with a supervisor reveals other opportunities for professional growth.

I will face my challenges head-on. It's only when I face them that I can see what I need to accept and what I can change.

As simple as possible

*"Everything should be made as simple as possible
. . . but not simpler."*

—⟶ ALBERT EINSTEIN

Whether it's an argument with a loved one, a
technological problem, a flawed work process,
or a personal inner conflict, life is full of opportunities for us to over-complicate our situation.
We need to look for the simplest solution,
but there is a danger of over-simplifying, too.
Feelings get hurt and we may do our work
poorly when we gloss over important details.

I can walk the balance between over-complicating
and over-simplifying a situation. There is a happy
medium where I can find the best path.

Learn by practicing

"The way you get better at playing football is to play football."

— GENE BRODIE

When we're doing something new, it's easy to get frustrated with our learning curve. All skills require learning and practice, and that can take time and be messy. We may look silly at first. We make mistakes. But, the only way we will improve is through instruction followed by practice—over and over. Eventually, we will get it right and be rewarded.

I will practice the new skills I am learning. I give myself permission to make mistakes and embrace my responsibility to keep trying.

Spending your time

"*Time is the coin of your life. It is the only coin you have, and only you can determine how it will be spent. Be careful lest you let other people spend it for you.*"

—⌕ CARL SANDBURG

Like anything in life, if we are not intentional about plotting and using our time, it will be used up by default. When we are passive about time management, we wind up governed by crises and other people's demands. We can't say "no," because we have not gone into the day with any requirements of our own. It is okay to spend our time on another's behalf—it can be an appropriate gift—but it is best when *we* make that choice.

I will be thoughtful and intentional in managing my time. I do not have to submit to pressure from others who want to take my time without asking.

A rainy afternoon

"Millions long for immortality who do not know what to do with themselves on a rainy Sunday afternoon."

—Susan Ertz

We all long for more time to do the things we love. Yet, when our day suddenly frees up and we have an afternoon to do absolutely anything, we draw a blank. What do we do now that our routine has disappeared?

Being hurried is so familiar; it feels awkward to have this empty canvas of time in front of us. What if we call a friend we haven't seen in a while? What if we read a good book? Maybe it's time to give ourselves a true break and take a nap! Whatever we do—or don't do—we can let go of the reins of routine for a few hours.

I welcome moments when I have no plans or my plans get cancelled. It's nice to take an extended break once in a while and simply do nothing.

Comfortable silence

> *"True friendship comes when silence between two people is comfortable."*

— 🕭 DAVE TYSON GENTRY

Early in relationships, we often feel we need to keep the conversation flowing. If there's too much silence, we wonder if the other person feels uncomfortable about something we said. We're not sure where they stand with us, and we're not sure what we think about them yet.

As we get to know each other, we feel secure in the relationship. There aren't anxious questions about whether a stop in the conversation means one of us is bothered by something. Silence between the two of us can simply mean we're sharing a restful moment together.

In some relationships, we can sit in the same room together in peaceful silence. The next time this happens, I will be grateful that I have a friendship that has reached this depth.

Danger and delight

"Danger and delight grow on one stalk."

— ENGLISH PROVERB

Our greatest pleasures often go hand-in-hand with great risk. Whether we are falling in love, riding a motorcycle, or learning to sail on the open ocean, our finest moments may involve confronting and claiming victory over something that is daunting or dangerous. We delight in overcoming danger.

I love to face fear and overcome it. I feel alive when I'm doing something that has an element of danger to it, and strong and confident when I've finished.

Accepting problems

"Anything in life that we don't accept will simply make trouble for us until we make peace with it."

—◌ SHAKTI GAWAIN

It seems counterintuitive: We need to accept a problem in order to solve it. As long as we refuse to accept the reality of the issue, we cannot deal with it. If we live in denial, an issue constantly comes back to haunt us or appears again in a sideways manner. If we are overly consumed with fighting it, the problem becomes our identity. It's only in acceptance that we find release and the possibility of change.

I can learn to accept my problems. I will peacefully acknowledge their reality, neither fighting nor pretending they don't exist.

Fear of decisions

*"We lose the fear of making decisions, great
and small, as we realize that should our choice
prove wrong, we can, if we will, learn from
the experience."*

— ANONYMOUS

No one is perfect, but as we carry on—making
decisions, making mistakes, finding success and
growing through it all—we mature. We get better at making decisions from practice. No experiences are wasted as long as we choose to learn
from all of them. It is always better to try our
best and make a useful mistake than to hide in
fear, making no decision and getting nowhere.

I give myself the freedom to make decisions—and
to make mistakes. I will learn a great deal in
the process.

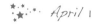

Shed your wrongdoings

"Shed, as you do your garments, your daily sins, whether of omission or commission, and you will wake a free man, with a new life."

—> SIR WILLIAM OSLER

We cannot change what we have or have not done today. We can only commit to a different action tomorrow and ask forgiveness wherever needed. Worrying long into the night will not help us solve a problem. We need to set aside those worries and enter the grace of sleep. It renews and restores us, and everything looks brighter in the morning.

As I change out of my daytime clothes, I will remove my concerns and errors and put them away, too. Whatever I have or have not done, I will let it all go as I sleep.

Surprises each day

"One never knows what each day is going to bring. The important thing is to be open and ready for it."

— HENRY MOORE

Tomorrow is full of possibilities. Who knows where it will take us? We can view each new day as a great adventure. With a sense of anticipation, we're less likely to be dragged down by our ordinary routine. In the midst of our day-to-day lives, there is magic and wonder if we are ready and watching.

I am ready for whatever comes tomorrow. In the morning, I will wake up both physically and spiritually eager to see what treasure I can find.

Character grows from habit

"Character is simply habit long enough continued."

— PLUTARCH

Persist in a certain practice for a couple of weeks and it becomes habit. Persist in it for a couple of months and it becomes hard *not* to do it. Keep at it for a couple of years and it changes who we are. Whatever the habit, good or not so good, it is a part of us—an expression of our values. How do others describe us? Picky, fun-loving, casual, fickle, introverted, honest, or intense? Others come to their conclusions about us through observing our habits.

My character is a composite of my habits. I will decide carefully about embracing new habits, breaking old ones, and choosing those I want to maintain.

Appreciate the climb

"Live your life each day as you would climb a mountain. An occasional glance toward the summit keeps the goal in mind, but many beautiful scenes are to be observed from each new vantage point. Climb slowly, steadily, enjoying each passing moment; and the view from the summit will serve as a fitting climax for the journey."

—HAROLD B. MELCHART

How sad it would be if we trekked up a mountain with a constant stream of complaints flowing from our mouths. By the time we got to the top, we would have worn ourselves out with grumbling—and dampened the spirits of our companions. Our attitude during the journey sets the stage for our feelings during life's high points. The journey is so beautiful; we must be careful not to miss all it has to offer.

I will traverse life's mountainsides with joy. When I succeed in reaching each summit, I will be even happier.

Riches

> "Who is rich? He that is content. Who is that? Nobody."
>
> —⌒ BENJAMIN FRANKLIN

Money definitely makes things easier. We all rest well at night when we know we can take care of our financial obligations. Has the car broken down? No problem, just bring it to the dealership—we have a "rainy day" fund set aside for that.

But we can run into trouble if we start believing that money and possessions define us. A good salary may cause us to stay in an unfulfilling career. We may become jealous of neighbors or family members because they own bigger homes or drive newer cars. We feel resentful when others receive handouts, while we have worked hard for our money.

I can think about money as something that helps me do good things for myself and others, not as a goal all by itself. Contentment comes from within, not from material possessions.

We need family

> "Call it a clan, call it a network, call it a tribe, call it a family; whatever you call it, whoever you are, you need one."
>
> —JANE HOWARD

We are social creatures, wired to live in relationships. Our identity can't come from work alone. We need social time and space, just as we need food and water. Even the most introverted among us need at least a few close friends with whom we can reflect, question, encourage, and support. It's in these safe relationships that we develop and define ourselves.

I will take care of my family and family-like relationships. We need each other. These relationships are the most important part of my life.

Work is worth its wage

> *The laboring man and the artificer knows what every hour of his time is worth, and parts not with it but for the full value.*

—— LORD CLARENDON

Homemakers and laborers alike know full well the value of their work. They spend their personal energy and creativity, hitting the end of each day exhausted. The effort that goes into each hour deserves appreciation.

We need to respect others' time at home and in the workplace, be cautious about expecting too many favors, and view our own time as valuable as well. We are spending our selves as we work; it's understandable that we want to be rewarded and acknowledged.

The time and effort that people put into their tasks deserves to be valued. I will keep a healthy respect for their time and mine.

Just ask

"Many things are lost for want of asking."
—◠ ENGLISH PROVERB

Sometimes opportunities are close enough to touch, yet we shy away. It seems too good to be true, or we're scared of taking the risk of speaking up. The worst that can happen, if we ask, is that we might be told "no." That's the same result as if we hadn't asked at all, so no harm done. Sometimes, however, we get what we ask for—but only if we make the request.

When I have a request to make, I will be courageous and ask it. I might be told "no." But, I might be told "yes." That can be life-changing.

Going against the flow

"Any intelligent fool can make things bigger, more complex, and more violent. It takes a touch of genius—and a lot of courage—to move in the opposite direction."

—⌂ E.F. SCHUMACHER

Whether it's an individual trying to get out of debt or nations trying to establish peace, it can be painful to clean up the messes we humans make. How easily we wander into trouble, creating complexities where there were none and inventing artificial emergencies.

It takes both genius and courage to walk against the flow of a world prone to creating stress. Choosing simplicity and peace begins with individual decisions. It begins in our homes and moves outward into the rest of the world.

I will have the courage to speak and act in a way that embraces simplicity and peace.

Self-discovery

"A single event can awaken within us a stranger totally unknown to us."

— ANTOINE DE SAINT-EXUPÉRY

It could be a significant crisis or a joyful high point, or it could be a humble moment of clarity while taking an evening walk. A drastic shift comes in our thinking and leaves us reeling with the choice of whether to become a new person or go back to the past.

How do we explain this new attitude to those around us? How do we explain it to ourselves? The answers are not easy, but we know we will never be the same. Decisive now, we embrace our new identity and the internal and outward change it brings.

There were many events in my life that were completely out of my control. I see how those times have shaped, challenged, and transformed me. Some moments have been especially hard, yet I found the strength to grow through them. I marvel at my story and at whom I am becoming.

Hard work

> "Opportunities are usually disguised as hard work, so most people don't recognize them."
>
> —ANN LANDERS

It's too hard; maybe it's just not meant to be. It is the most common excuse to avoid an opportunity disguised as a challenge. The silver platter arrives, it's placed on our lap, but what lies scattered atop is the upended contents of a puzzle—and it seems someone has made off with the box! Potentially grand and beautiful yes, but suddenly we realize our dream is going to require thought and energy.

We can't let that moment of re-evaluation discourage us or cause us to shrink. Now is the time to commit wholly to the challenge. We need to take care of ourselves physically, emotionally, and spiritually to ensure we have the energy and creativity to face what is at hand.

The challenge I'm facing is different from others I've had. But I know I have the skills and experience needed to succeed.

Fearless focus

"*Become so wrapped up in something that you
forget to be afraid.*"

—◦ LADY BIRD JOHNSON

We hear it in the voice of a hero interviewed
at an accident scene. The reporter asks, "But
weren't you afraid?" Weren't they afraid of the
flames, the car wreck, the steep terrain? The
answer is always something similar. "No, I just
did what anyone would do in the same situation. I didn't have time to be afraid."

This kind of focus doesn't need a crisis to
exist. There are many other moments that are not
life-or-death scenarios, such as facing a deadline,
a daunting creative task, or a complex relationship. We can tap into a focus so strong that fear
no longer clouds our judgment.

I choose to focus wholly on this task or relationship and my hopes for it, so that I no longer have
the space to fret over my fears.

Truly alive

" *To live is so startling it leaves little time for anything else.* "

—⁂ EMILY DICKINSON

It's easy to fill our lives with mundane and petty urgencies. Time managers describe life as a glass jar, into which we place sand, pebbles, and larger stones. Many elements of our daily routine qualify as sand. Love, relationships, and a robust sense of wonder are the stones that are difficult to fit in the jar if we let sand fill it up first.

Make time for life-filled activities first. Is it pragmatic? Honestly, not always. A few to-do list items may get lost in the shuffle. The adjustment may be awkward, but our life becomes richer, our mind more alert, and we are happier as we complete our other tasks.

Releasing all my concerns, I take this moment to reflect in wonder and gratitude—to live.

Importance of play

"The true object of all human life is play."

—G.K. CHESTERTON

Sometimes we think of play as frivolous. As adults, we get to play occasionally in our sports, hobbies, romance, or time with the children in our lives. How often is that play hindered by the distractions of deadlines and other time constraints?

The side effects of play are organic learning and growth. In play, we let our minds wander and dream up new ideas. Play brings fresh energy into our lives and helps us discover new ways to move. It is part of the delightful ties we have with others.

I welcome a playful spirit in my life, work, and relationships.

Investing in others

> "*Time and money spent in helping men to do more for themselves is far better than mere giving.*"
>
> —⌀ HENRY FORD

Giving money to help a problem in society does offer a temporary fix. To give in a way that equips and transforms an individual in need is the beginning of real change. It requires more creativity and, often, more time and effort, but it is far more rewarding for all involved. Whether we decide to give our time through mentorship or pro bono work, or research charities until we find one that empowers the people it serves, those extra efforts reap a valuable harvest.

I will invest in other people in ways that effect lasting change.

The treasure of kindness

"Guard well within yourself that treasure, kindness. Know how to give without hesitation, how to lose without regret, how to acquire without meanness."

—— GEORGE SAND

Too often, we approach giving with a "what's in it for me" attitude. We extend a hand to a colleague only if we think we may someday receive a favor in return. We lend money to friends, and expect to be paid back with interest. We volunteer for professional or neighborhood duties to advance our careers or protect and enhance the value of our homes. Our minds are always focused on what we are gaining or losing.

But there are no rewards for true kindness, nor is there any reason for our happiness to decrease by being shared. A kind heart is like a candle that can used to light dozens of others, without losing any of its own flame.

Even if my kindness isn't returned, I will be stronger for living up to my principles.

Ordinary spirituality

"In order to experience everyday spirituality, we need to remember that we are spiritual beings spending some time in a human body."

—BARBARA DE ANGELIS

Routines and day-to-day tasks can become so dominant and pressing that we forget who we are. Sometimes, we compartmentalize our lives so much that spirituality is just an item on our list, a task we attend to only at certain moments. We are spiritual creatures no matter what we are doing. Acts of faith and consciousness are not meant to be fragments detached from the rest of "real life."

We can bring our awareness up a notch, treating our everyday routines as living prayers. We open our eyes, just a little bit, and begin to see that every moment is imbued with spiritual truth.

I am beginning to see how ordinary life is steeped in spirituality. I will open my eyes a little more each day.

Logic and faith

> **"***If we were logical, the future would be bleak indeed. But we are more than logical. We are human beings, and we have faith, and we have hope.***"**

—○ JACQUES COUSTEAU

Facts and data can indicate that we've gotten ourselves between a rock and a hard place. History resonates with stories of people who have been in similar predicaments, yet refused to become discouraged and found a surprising way out. It doesn't require denying logic and facts; it is an act of transcending the facts.

Hope is sure that there is one last overlooked angle, one miniscule movement that will make all the difference. We are infinitely resourceful and creative when we let ourselves be.

There are situations in my world that are very discouraging. I choose to regard them with a sense of hope. I will be attentive, watching for that overlooked solution.

Faith dismantles fear

"*Fear imprisons, faith liberates; fear paralyzes, faith empowers; fear disheartens, faith encourages; fear sickens, faith heals; fear makes useless, faith makes serviceable.*"

—⟶ HARRY EMERSON FOSDICK

The opposite of faith isn't doubt or skepticism. In fact, the process of questioning often leads to faith. Fear is the force that really eats away at faith. When we focus on our fears, we get stuck. We build walls of protection that keep us "safe" but totally isolated and unable to move.

When we let even the smallest grain of faith take root in our souls, its growth begins to wear away and crumble the stone of fear. We become flexible and creative again. We see possibilities and we heal.

I encourage faith to grow in my heart and delight in faith's ability to break down fear.

Know your convictions

"We should know what our convictions are, and stand for them. Upon one's own philosophy, conscious or unconscious, depends one's ultimate interpretation of facts. Therefore it is wise to be as clear as possible about one's subjective principles. As the man is, so will be his ultimate truth."

—CARL JUNG

We make value judgments throughout each day, often without considering where our assumptions come from and whether they are grounded in fact or not. It takes more work to examine our principles and honestly assess our beliefs, but it's much more satisfying. Breaking free from autopilot, we can question our own ideas and release ourselves to adjust and grow.

I am developing well-grounded principles and my own life philosophy. I will test my thoughts and assumptions to make sure they are valid, then take a solid stand on these convictions.

Take hold of happiness

"Happiness hates the timid!"

— EUGENE O'NEILL

Our feelings can be influenced by circumstances outside our control. Over the long term, however, we have a large amount of choice about how we feel. Our daily decisions to direct our inner thoughts toward sad matters or hopeful ones reinforce one emotion or the other.

Happy people tend to possess an ingrained habit of looking for the good in any moment; one bit of happiness creates more happiness. It takes a strong will to direct one's thoughts in this fashion.

I boldly take hold of happiness. Whenever my thoughts turn sad or discouraging, I will insist on looking for one thing I can be happy about and meditate on it.

Encouragement from within

"*You can enjoy encouragement coming from outside, but you cannot need for it to come from outside.*"

— VLADIMIR ZWORYKIN

It feels fantastic to hear encouraging words, whether they come from a coach, boss, or loved one. It gives us a boost and the inspiration to continue on our journey. It's even better to have a sense of certainty that comes from within. Setting and reaching a goal or completing a big project requires inner strength and approval. We can draw on that, even when some of our usual cheerleaders have become silent.

I am my own greatest encouragement. I will speak encouraging words to myself about a challenge in my life right now.

Make yourself strong

❝*We either make ourselves miserable, or we make ourselves strong. The amount of work is the same.*❞

—⤳ CARLOS CASTANEDA

It takes a lot of creativity to keep finding the negative spin on our circumstances. It actually takes more muscle effort to frown than to let our faces relax into a pleasant smile. We spend energy every day on our thought processes and emotional patterns. We can choose to turn that energy toward a positive focus.

People who focus on the good in every situation tend to have a greater sense of gratitude and are more resourceful. They see what they have at hand and are quick to use it. Their character is strengthened because they do not open themselves to defeat and despair.

I choose to strengthen myself by focusing on the positive. I will look for the good in my life and enjoy it!

Personal opinion

> *Though reading and conversation may furnish us with many ideas of men and things, our own meditation must form our judgment.*
>
> —ᗉ ISAAC WATTS

When we hear or read the opinions of a person we admire, we may want to agree with all they have to say without thinking about it. When we hear something that seems a little "off," we're not sure whether to question it. We can allow ourselves to consider the sticky point. Where is the dissonance coming from? What might be a better approach?

It is good to find people whose wisdom we can trust. It's even better when we realize we can disagree and still treat each other with respect.

I enjoy learning from others. I also delight in forming my own judgment on the matters that affect me and my world.

Small actions, big impact

"We are here to change the world with small acts of thoughtfulness done daily rather than with one great breakthrough."

—⮾ RABBI HAROLD KUSHNER

The world's troubles hang heavy on our shoulders. The evening news can be an overwhelming glimpse into pain and suffering. How can we even begin to make a difference? Being overwhelmed can leave us paralyzed, doing nothing because it all just seems too big.

All it takes is a quick shift of focus to the one small thing that we can do right now. That small thing—a cup of coffee for a co-worker, a hug and word of encouragement to a loved one, a small gift to a favorite charity—can mean the world to the recipient. It also opens us up, helps us stretch, and tends to release a wellspring of even more simple, gentle, meaningful acts.

My thoughtful actions won't save the whole world, but they may make a real difference for a few people right now. That matters.

Unity of body and soul

"The body too has its rights; and it will have them: they cannot be trampled on without peril. The body ought to be the soul's best friend."

—◌ AUGUSTUS WILLIAM HARE AND
JULIUS CHARLES HARE
(CO-AUTHORS)

Choices to work late, skip meals, and rarely exercise—they add up. Just ask the office manager who gave 30 years of high-stress company loyalty and recently needed triple bypass surgery, or the graphic artist who burned the midnight oil for a big account and then came down with the flu.

How smoothly life would go if we simply befriended our bodies, treated them with respect, and honored them with a sane lifestyle and gentle care.

I enjoy living life in a way that honors my own body. I will think of ways I can care for myself— and do them.

Infinite love

"*God loves each of us as if there were only one of us.*"

—⌁ SAINT AUGUSTINE

We get a glimpse of infinite love within families. When parents are fair, kind, and accept the individuality of each family member, their children are less likely to feel emotionally isolated—and don't feel the need to vie for parental approval.

It is much the same with our Creator. Though our faith communities are diverse, God's fairness and eternal love leads each of us to feel uniquely blessed. Because we live by the same set of divine principles, we find ourselves on equal footing with our brothers and sisters in faith.

There is only one person on the planet exactly like me. God delights in me and loves me exactly as I am.

Go straight at things

"I believe half the unhappiness in life comes from people being afraid to go straight at things."

— WILLIAM J. LOCK

When we are not honest with ourselves and others, we cause our own internal dissonance. As soon as we face an issue straight on and use plain language to talk about it, no matter how awkward or scary the process is, we have taken a step toward resolution. Once we name the thing and discuss it, we can discover what parts of the problem we can change and what parts we will need to let go. We no longer have to keep wondering "what if." Now, we are ready to find serenity and true happiness.

It can be scary to be straightforward about a problem, but I have the courage to do this. I will face issues and discuss them with honesty and respect. Through that choice, I open the door to improvement and happiness.

Obstacles as guides

"The obstacle is the path."

— ZEN PROVERB

We grow by stretching ourselves, trying something we've never done before. When we take those risks, we are clumsy and run into unfamiliar obstacles. Then we need more learning and research, taking us on yet another new journey. In this way, our path is a string of obstacles, each one building on the one before and leading to the next.

Where to go now? We take our cues from the questions we're struggling with at the moment. There is the path. Find the answer.

Obstacles aren't necessarily bad. I can use them as guideposts along my path, showing me where I need to go next and what I need to learn.

Pursuit of happiness

> *"The U.S. Constitution doesn't guarantee happiness, only the pursuit of it. You have to catch up with it yourself."*

—⌒ BENJAMIN FRANKLIN

Our government, culture, family, or social circle can't bring happiness to us. Happiness is not an event or a state that happens to us; it's something we must run after, grasp, and then plant and cultivate in ourselves. This pursuit is an ongoing process and there will always be parts of our life in which we have to start the pursuit over and over again. Our understanding of happiness evolves as we mature and better understand ourselves.

I choose to pursue happiness within myself, rather than expecting any other entity to provide it for me.

Everything has a time

> "Have a time and a place for everything, and do everything in its time and place, and you will not only accomplish more, but have far more leisure than those who are always hurrying."
>
> —⁏ TYRON EDWARDS

The great time-management truth is that there are always urgent little issues in life clamoring for our attention. The key to *having* time for leisure, rest, and activities with our loved ones is simply to *make* the time. Set the time aside and use it. We will renew ourselves and be present with those we love.

We come away from our rest, leisure, and time with loved ones re-energized. As a side effect, we wind up accomplishing more because we can think more clearly and make decisions with a level mind.

I will make time for the things that matter and respect those commitments as sacred.

Friendship is an art

"*Friendship is an art, and very few persons are born with a natural gift for it.*"

— KATHLEEN NORRIS

Some people really are naturals at being good friends. For most of us, it is a learned skill. As with any art, we may have some talent, but we have to learn the basics first. We are not born knowing that it's good to make regular phone calls just to check up on a friend, send a care package, or host a dinner. We often don't know what to say when a friend is going through a hard time or understand that sometimes nothing at all needs to be said; a hug is good enough. With time and a willingness to ask our friends what they need, we learn and begin to practice real friendship.

I am learning how to be a good friend. I am willing to take a lesson from my friends, to share my needs with them and ask about theirs. I'll practice the art of friendship.

The daily grind

"Most of life is routine—dull and grubby, but routine is the mountain that keeps a man going. If you wait for inspiration you'll be standing on the corner after the parade is a mile down the street."

—▸ BEN NICHOLAS

Routine can be so boring. Yet, to achieve a goal or foster a certain attitude, we must create a routine. Not only do we do our basic self-care each morning, we also write for half an hour in a journal because we've noticed it puts us in a better mood for the rest of the day. When we have a year-long project, we know we can break it down into routine bite-sized portions that we complete each day. Routine is the framework we use to keep our pace and take our lives in the direction we've chosen.

Routine isn't bad. I see that some routines have really helped me in the past. I will continue to use and adjust my routine to create a life that works well for me.

Good old days

"Let others praise ancient times; I am glad I was born in these."

—ꙮ OVID (81 B.C.)

Even the people of antiquity were accustomed to hearing others reminisce about "the good old days." We are always looking back and thinking things were better then. Remembering how things used to be and missing the good things that were a part of the past, we can only think of what we've lost.

We can experience good times now, too. There are people today who share our values, even if the expression of those values may look different. Our longing for yesterday should not overshadow the richness and beauty of today.

I am thankful to be alive in today's world. There are unique blessings and experiences that I can only have because I am living in this time and place.

Don't delay doing right

" *The time is always right to do what is right.* **"**

—⁂ MARTIN LUTHER KING, JR.

There's no sense in procrastinating about doing the right thing. It may be risky to stand up for what we believe, but the greater risk is remaining silent and inactive. When we do nothing, we have forfeited our right to act. We're letting someone else have control.

I will do the right thing. I won't delay any longer.

Mountainsides

"To live only for some future goal is shallow. It's the sides of the mountain that sustain life, not the top."

—⌒ ROBERT M. PIRSIG

Goals are invigorating and dreams are precious. The route along the way is where we do our living. If we only live in the future, we may miss the beautiful view right where we are. Taking a break to enjoy this moment won't hurt our momentum in getting to the summit. If anything, it will energize us.

Attitudes grow and solidify in the grittiness of daily life. A constantly future-oriented mind has a hard time appreciating the grand goal, even when it's accomplished. When we teach ourselves to slow down and enjoy today, we ensure that we will be ready to appreciate our goal when we finally attain it.

I don't want my goals to be my only driving force. I'll open my eyes and appreciate the path.

Sleep on it

"It is a common experience that a problem difficult at night is resolved in the morning after the committee of sleep has worked on it."

— JOHN STEINBECK

What is it that happens to us overnight that allows things to come into such sharp focus in the morning? Whatever occurs biochemically, it works. What a mercy it is to "sleep on it." We feel worn out right now, and that colors our perspective. We can release ourselves to rest; we're not going to solve all the problems of the world tonight. In the morning, we'll have the energy and clarity to think it through. We'll also have a better ability to figure out which parts of the problem are truly our responsibility.

I can let myself sink into sleep now. Staying up won't make my problem solve itself sooner; it might even make it loom worse in my thoughts. I release it now, trusting that it will be much clearer in the morning with a well-rested mind.

Perfectionism

> " *There are those who are so scrupulously afraid of doing wrong that they seldom venture to do anything.* "

—⟳ VAUVENARGUES

Perfectionism can be paralyzing. Afraid to mess up, we find it impossible to try anything new. Instead of limiting ourselves to a familiar routine where everything is under control, we can be kind to ourselves and welcome the opportunity to learn and make mistakes. Trying something new, we're bound to be messy, but we'll get so much out of it as we stretch our thinking.

It's fine for me to make mistakes—and I know I will as I explore the unfamiliar. I will let go of my perfectionism so I'm free to try something new.

Asking what if

"A dreamer—you know—it's a mind that looks over the edges of things."

—✏ MARY O'HARA

The daydreaming mind asks, "What would happen if . . . ?" It also doodles with thought, following no specific path. Perhaps as children, we were told not to daydream. It was considered lazy. The dreamer knows that much can be accomplished in that seemingly frivolous time. The oddest musings bubble to the surface while daydreaming. When we let our curiosity and creativity come out to play, we increase the likelihood that we'll have clever ideas throughout our routine hours.

I need time to let my mind wander, dream, and wonder, "What if?" Letting myself dream, I give myself permission to entertain any idea and possibility.

Freedom and security

> *"Free man is by necessity insecure; thinking man by necessity uncertain."*

—⟲ ERICH FROMM

Sometimes we are frightened by freedom. Though we are responsible for our choices, we have no control over the many variables. The element of randomness in life can be unsettling.

We can arrange our plans and decisions perfectly, only to have them changed in an instant. The more we think about a decision, the more aware we become of contingencies. It can be overwhelming. It is both humbling and invigorating to know we are responsible for the choices in our little part of the greater story. We will navigate the contingencies and learn to use the changing tide to our advantage.

My freedom results in a high degree of uncertainty. The future is not secure. But it is mine to explore and navigate. I will hold all my plans loosely.

Fighting too hard

"Resistance causes pain and lethargy. It is when we practice acceptance that new possibilities appear."

—— ANONYMOUS

When an obstacle appears in our lives, initially we want to fight it. Hard. We take a militant approach; we want this problem gone. But it isn't. All our efforts seem futile, and we recognize we're wearing ourselves out repeatedly trying the same tactic.

Finally, we come back to acceptance. It feels like we're giving up. We're not. We're just recognizing reality and being honest with ourselves. Gently, we accept what's in front of us. Then, as if by magic, we can see a completely different way over, around, or through the issue.

Whenever I get the feeling that I'm fighting a little too hard, I will remember to look at the problem and simply accept what it is.

A new day tomorrow

> *"Snow endures but for a season, and joy comes with the morning."*
>
> —⟡ MARCUS AURELIUS

Whatever we are going through, we know it will not last forever. There will be a new season, a fresh change. Meanwhile, we can take comfort in the miniature fresh start we have in each new day.

Struggles and dull times come to an end. Whatever happened to me today, I can look forward to a new day tomorrow. I am thankful for the days and the seasons; they remind me that nothing lasts forever.

Listening to desires

"Never let go of that fiery sadness called desire."
—PATTI SMITH

Our first instinct is to want to remedy our desires—to meet them or decide against entertaining them. Unmet desire is frustrating. Once desire is met, we may be surprised that the initial desire only led to another. Are we insatiable, or simply human?

All our longings taken together are like pieces in the puzzle of our life. When we check in with our unmet desires, we find hints at how to recreate ourselves. We also find unending fuel for the journey. Our goal is not satisfying the desire as much as valuing the process of getting there.

There is so much I long for in life. I will take my desires seriously, listening to them for clues about where to go next.

Right now

> *"The present moment is significant, not as the bridge between past and future, but by reason of its contents, which can fill our emptiness and become ours, if we are capable of receiving them."*

—∽ DAG HAMMARSKJÖLD

The mind is constantly simmering with thoughts. Usually, these are thoughts about what has already happened or what we need to do next to fulfill a want or need. Once in a while, we are present in the right now. We have experienced those rare "moments of being," perhaps as we conversed with a loved one, enjoyed nature, or participated in a creative or athletic activity.

Completely present, we lose track of time. We discover this moment is all we need.

I will rest into this moment right now.

Wishbone or backbone?

"Never grow a wishbone, daughter, where your backbone ought to be."

— CLEMENTINE PADDLEFORD

Wasting our time wishing can become a habit. The more we let our minds wander into wishing, the less we remember to take action. There's only one way to see a hope turn into reality: decide on the first small step and then take it.

We need the perseverance to keep at it, to keep envisioning the next small step. Just as our bodies are strengthened by exercise, the backbone of our will is strengthened through regular practice.

I have a strong backbone. I have the resolve to turn my dreams into reality.

Liking yourself

“*I've learned to take time for myself and to treat myself with a great deal of love and respect 'cause I like me . . . I think I'm kind of cool.*”

—⟶ WHOOPI GOLDBERG

Two women were chatting one day. One was being critical of herself, mulling over an area in her life where she felt she didn't measure up. The other woman interrupted and said, "Hey, you be nice to my friend! I like her; you should, too."

Apt words. It's good to press the mute button on the inner critic and remember we are precious. Even when others are not there to remind us to be gentle with ourselves, we can speak some kind words and be our own good friend, and treat ourselves with love and respect.

I am worthy of my own respect, care, and delight. I find myself interesting and fun.

Care for your body

"*What fools indeed we mortals are*
To lavish care upon a Car,
With ne'er a bit of time to see
About our own machinery!"

—⟶ JOHN KENDRICK BANGS

Sometimes our lives get unbalanced. We all know people who put more time into the care of their possessions than into care for themselves. There are times when we've done it, too. It's not a bad thing to take pride in the things we care about, but it's more important to give our physical bodies TLC.

I will look at how I'm spending my time. There are small ways to change the rhythm of my life so I take more time to care for my body.

Responding to criticism

"Criticism may not be agreeable, but it is necessary. It fulfills the same function as pain in the human body. It calls attention to an unhealthy state of things."

— WINSTON CHURCHILL

Criticism feels uncomfortable, and it may take effort to sift through it and discern whether the critical words were well founded. Or, maybe they were undue and harsh, indicating that the "unhealthy state of things" was in the speaker's hands. Often, it's a mix of both.

Deciding how we'll respond—whether we'll make a change, ignore it for now, or request that the other cease and desist—are all difficult choices. In any event, the experience gets our attention and makes us a little more alert to our situation and relationships.

I don't enjoy hearing criticism, but I appreciate the wrestling, learning, and growth that come as a result.

Saying and doing

> "*Between saying and doing many pairs of shoes are worn out.*"
>
> —⟲ ITALIAN PROVERB

Every day we have thoughts and conversations about what we hope to do someday or about how we wish a situation would change for the better. We can get stuck at talk. It's a big commitment to be the change—but how satisfying it is. Months or years down the line, we can look back and say, "I made that happen."

I can look back at periods when I dedicated time and effort to a cause. It was satisfying work. There are areas in my life and community that call for a similar dedication right now. It's time to take action.

Love is a need

> *"The hunger for love is much more difficult to remove than the hunger for bread."*
>
> —◌ MOTHER TERESA

Our need for love is just as vital as our need for food. People thrive only through the satisfaction of both physical and spiritual needs. The pace of our schedules—set in motion to provide for our own bread—often makes it difficult to give of ourselves. Can't we just make a financial donation to a charity? Isn't it easier to buy a gift for our friend? Thankfully, deep inside, we are not satisfied until we are giving and receiving meaningful acts of love.

I have the time to love and be loved. It is just as important as caring for basic needs.

Lead from behind

"To lead people, walk behind them."

—— LAO TZU

Sometimes leaders seem out of touch with the people they are guiding. We've all experienced the dissonance this creates, whether we were members of a work team or family, or leaders ourselves.

When we are in leadership roles, one quick way to restore connection is to lead from behind. Watch, listen, and take time to follow people to learn about their strengths, abilities, needs, and opinions. With that knowledge, we're able to make decisions that show our willingness to help the people in our care do their parts.

When I am in a leadership role, I will look at where my group is and discover more about each member's role and what they need to do a good job.

Hold expectations loosely

> "Expect nothing. Live frugally on surprise."
> —∾ ALICE WALKER

We set goals. We make plans. We have many hopes and dreams. But life is unpredictable. Changes are inevitable. Those surprises can jar and frustrate us, or they can be part of a grand adventure.

It is possible to hold our plans loosely. When we do this, we are able to move forward on the path we've chosen, but if an interesting alternative shows up, we're less likely to brush it off as a distraction. It doesn't bother us so much if a roadblock comes up. In fact, it can be fun. Like a child, we exclaim in surprise, "Oh, I wonder what I'll do instead."

I'll make plans, but I won't be rigid about my expectations. I can hold my schedule loosely, always ready to receive a surprise.

Love is the guiding principle

"Love, and do what you like."

—⌒ SAINT AUGUSTINE

Most spiritual traditions come back to something that sounds like the Golden Rule. When we choose, act, and live in love, we really can't go wrong. First embracing a loving attitude toward others and ourselves, it naturally follows that we will not harm anyone. Even more, we will take steps to increase our sense of connection and offer help and encouragement to all those around us.

The most important part of my life is my capacity for love. I will focus on love and let everything else flow out from that center.

A process of elimination

> "*The sculptor produces the beautiful statue by chipping away such parts of the marble block as are not needed—it is a process of elimination.*"
>
> —ⒼⒼ ELBERT HUBBARD

Sculptors often speak of freeing their work from within the raw material. Sometimes we are like that work in progress, too. We can be our own artists, seeing through the raw material to the self we wish to be.

It is hard work, chipping away at the stone. We begin to say "no" and prune away past commitments that aren't appropriate for us. We give away old clothes and change our physical space. We cultivate healthier friendships. Slowly, chip-by-chip, the new self takes shape.

I can use a creative process of elimination as I design a healthier lifestyle. This is a helpful metaphor for any big decision, too.

Take risks, live fully

> *The proper function of man is to live, not to exist. I shall not waste my days in trying to prolong them.*

—JACK LONDON

While it's wise to care for our bodies and take precautions when doing something dangerous, it's possible to be too careful. It is refreshing and life-giving to dive fully into life, to take a few extravagant risks and experience the rush of feeling completely alive. We were meant to live, not just preserve ourselves. If we're too cautious, we will get to the end of our lives wondering if we missed out.

I will take the risk of living life fully. I might try hiking a difficult mountain trail or take up a contact sport. Whatever I do, it will be an invigorating challenge. I will embrace it completely.

Never a dull moment

"The most important thing in our lives is what we are doing now."

— ⌐ ANONYMOUS

What if what we're doing right now is rather dull? Does it really matter? Yes; the present moment, whatever it is, is the most vital. Right now is the only second we can orchestrate. Now is the moment when we can decide on our perspective. When we realize this, we breathe new life into all our activities.

We have no idea what might happen even five minutes from now, and we can do nothing to change the past. Whether we are cozy in our bed, sitting in a coffee shop, brushing our teeth, or on an airplane longing for the comforts of home—this moment, what we are doing right now, matters. Even the most ordinary acts simmer with who we are, right now.

I am vital and present in every moment, no matter how exciting or mundane. I will breathe and marvel at who I am and what I am doing right now.

Listening ear

"Listen long enough and the person will generally come up with an adequate solution."

—⌖ MARY KAY ASH

We're usually a little too quick with advice. Unsolicited advice can be unwelcome, and can come off as condescending. Unless friends are in danger, it's best to act as a sounding board, to let them talk through their problems and find the answers on their own. We can remember when someone was a listening ear for us. The best part was how, all of a sudden, the solution appeared in our mind's eye. Talking about the problem made the solution clear. When we're the one listening, we can restrain ourselves and let others discover their own solution.

I don't have to give advice right away when friends and family talk to me about a problem. I can just listen and celebrate with them when they realize what they need to do.

Worry

> "*Who of you by worrying can add a single hour to his life? Since you cannot do this very little thing, why do you worry about the rest?*"

—◌ JESUS

We can chew on a problem for hours without finding a remedy. The mind is overwhelmed by all the contingencies. What if I try this, and then this happens . . . what then? Whether the bone we gnaw on is relational, financial, creative, or some deep personal frustration, we achieve little by worrying.

Is it so vital that we find a solution right now? Tomorrow may bring answers we had not seen before.

I release my worries and permit myself to rest. I will focus on my breathing and remember that tomorrow will bring its own solutions.

Trust your hunches

"Trust your hunches . . . hunches are usually based on facts filed away just below the conscious level. Warning! Do not confuse your hunches with wishful thinking. This is the road to disaster."

— DR. JOYCE BROTHERS

Our instincts often have logic to them. They usually are a by-product of facts that we are aware of subconsciously. In the moment, we simply know what we must do. After the fact, when we have time, we reason through it and see the unconscious logic behind our hunch.

We must be careful to not confuse instinct with wishful thought. Instinct has a solid urgency and possesses a seed of wisdom; wishful thinking tends toward fickle urges and a denial of the truth. Knowing the difference between the two and then honing our instincts comes through constant practice.

Relying on hunches sounds unsteady, but I recognize the deep intelligence in my hunches. I can think of many times when my hunches have been correct.

Selective forgetting

"Not the power to remember, but its very opposite, the power to forget, is a necessary condition for our existence."

—— SHOLEM ASCH

If we remembered every stimulus that we came in contact with, it would affect our mental health. Relationships would rarely last more than a few days if we remembered every bothersome thing about our friends or loved ones. Walking down a busy city street would overwhelm us if we memorized every second of the experience. Our memories are amazing, but our ability to selectively forget is just as astounding. It makes our wide range of experience and relationships possible.

The next time I forget my keys, I won't get quite so upset with myself for having a poor memory. My ability to forget may annoy me once in a while, but I also recognize it as a great gift.

Hidden anger has greater power

> *"Anger as soon as fed is dead, 'tis starving makes it fat."*
>
> —— EMILY DICKINSON

Anger can be scary, but its power is the greatest when we keep it inside. Once we find an appropriate way to let it out, it usually disappears on its own. There are lots of physical activities that help process anger. We might go for a walk, dance to music on the radio, do a home improvement project, or sing outloud. Sometimes just talking about it to a friend does the trick.

Finally acknowledged, expressed, and released, the anger dissipates like a tendril of smoke. We're surprised. That wasn't so bad. Now we can think clearly again.

I won't hold on to anger. I'll express it appropriately, then decide with a clear mind whether there is anything constructive I can do about the situation.

Coming out of our caves

> *"Those who cannot give friendship will rarely receive it, and never hold it."*
>
> —⟡ DAGOBERT D. RUNES

To have friends, we must first be one. During times when friendship is scarce, it's tempting to hole up in our little caves and wait for others to make the first move. What about our needs? How can we give friendship when we're feeling a little starved ourselves? As soon as we take the risk of reaching out with a few caring gestures, someone responds positively. We find ourselves forging a new friendship.

It takes effort to reach out in friendship, but I know my effort will be rewarded. I will take the risk of being a good friend.

Cherishing children

❝ *Most convicted felons are just people who were not taken to museums or Broadway musicals as children.* ❞

—⌥ LIBBY GELMAN-WAXNER

Children need to have their basic needs met, but we've seen the damage done when that is the *only* thing they receive. Whether growing up without parents or in a home where the parents are emotionally absent, kids who do not learn love at an early age may have a hard time later. They don't all become criminals, of course, but they sometimes struggle emotionally later in life.

We must look out for the well-being of the children in our lives, not only to ensure their physical needs are covered, but to make sure they are cherished. We do this by spending time with them, engaging in the world with them, and, of course, saying, "I love you."

The children in my life are precious. When I teach them love and consideration, I am influencing how our society will look decades from now.

The power of kindness

"Kindness affects more than severity."

—— AESOP

When we're in the wrong, it makes it harder to change our opinion when someone is lecturing us. We feel defensive because it sounds like they not only take issue with our ideas, they take issue with *us*. We stand tough, holding to our opinion even if we wonder if it might be wrong.

We can remember how that feels when we want to educate someone else about their poor behavior or flawed ideas. Speaking in a condescending or cruel tone will go nowhere. When we use a tone of genuine kindness and concern for the other's well-being, we are much more likely to win their good opinion—of our thoughts and of ourselves.

I will season my words with kindness whenever I am taking issue with someone.

We all need help

"Everyone needs help from everyone."

—⬡ BERTOLT BRECHT

Needing help doesn't mean we're helpless, it means we're human. We can graciously ask for and receive help. When we're on the receiving end, we learn invaluable lessons about how we can treat others when we're helping them. We can be more sensitive to how they feel when they admit they need help. Letting them know that we've been there, we build a bridge of relationship, empathy, and encouragement. That's the greatest help of all—the knowledge that we are not alone.

I'm not meant to live life as an island. I need help sometimes. At other times, I'm in a position where I can give help. I will do both with grateful connection.

Forgiveness is a choice

"*Forgiveness is an act of the will, and the will can function regardless of the temperature of the heart.*"

— CORRIE TEN BOOM

Sometimes we wait to forgive because we want to do it only when we feel ready. But forgiveness is actually a choice, something we do on principle. It's not a feeling, although our feelings will be affected by this powerful choice. Over time, as we choose to forgive each day, we begin to see our emotions loosen up and follow suit.

I will practice forgiveness. I realize it is a choice and a skill, and like any skill, it may not come naturally at first.

When change bothers others

"That's the risk you take if you change: that people you've been involved with won't like the new you. But other people who do will come along."

— LISA ALTHER

What if my best friend thinks I'm crazy for taking up this new hobby? What would my buddies do if I quit this bad habit? How will my relatives respond if I admit I've embraced views different from theirs? Change is scary enough as it is. When we factor in the response of others, it can be daunting. That must not hold us back. We can be sure we will meet new people who support and take interest in our new perspective.

Some of the people I know and love right now may not fully support changes I'm making. I still need to let myself grow and change. Somehow, we'll work things out. I'll make new friends as I proceed, too.

Feeling grumpy

"We have no more right to put our discordant states of mind into the lives of those around us and rob them of their sunshine and brightness than we have to enter their houses and steal their silverware."

— JULIA SETON

We have a bad day, and boy, do we feel grumpy! At home or with friends, we take it out on those around us. Soon they're having a rough day, too. That's not fair to them. It's fine to let people know we're feeling off, sad, or frustrated. It's not right to destroy their day just because ours isn't going right.

We must use self-control to deal appropriately with our emotions. We can learn to laugh at our circumstances and at ourselves. With that attitude, we can transform a bad day into a good one—for us and our loved ones.

I have bad days sometimes. That's normal. I will be careful not to bring everyone else down, too.

Family of choice

"Friends are the family we choose for ourselves."
—◌ EDNA BUCHANAN

Perhaps we were blessed with a family that nourished us and equipped us well as we grew up. Perhaps our family was riddled with sadness and difficulty. Whatever the case, we can have a wealth of family-like friendships. Other people can be as close as a sister, brother, mother, or father to us. We can return that blessing as well. In those relationships, we grow and learn even more about what it means to care for and support each other as a family.

I am so grateful for the friends I have who are like family to me. I will nourish those relationships and increase my ability to give and receive love.

Little advantages

"Happiness is produced not so much by great pieces of good fortune that seldom happen, as by little advantages that occur every day."

— ⤳ BENJAMIN FRANKLIN

It's true that the most lasting and satisfying changes are accomplished one tiny bit at a time. It's not winning the lottery as much as learning to save a little each month. It's not reaching the end of a project as much as our attitude and strategy along the way. It's not a sudden breakthrough in a relationship as much as the kind attitude we have started to cultivate each day.

Happiness is centered in ordinary life. It's not a lofty concept we'll enjoy only once we experience some far-off ideal. It is the little treasures hidden in every day.

I am happy as I reflect on today's unique gifts, experiences, and progress.

When will things be ideal?

"_The ideal never comes. Today is the ideal for him who makes it so._**"**

—↷ HORATIO W. DRESSER

What is our ideal, our "happily ever after?" Maybe it doesn't sound like a fairy tale, but it probably starts with, "Everything will be a lot better when …" It might be when we buy a house, get a promotion, reach a certain age, or see our loved ones achieve a certain milestone. What we don't always realize is that we will have a new set of challenges and limitations when we reach that far-off goal. Having goals is important, but our sense of peace rests in our ability to appreciate and fully experience all we have today.

When I stop to think about it, I realize I have a lot going for me today. My hopes and dreams are wonderful, but I won't let them prevent me from seeing everything that is ideal right now.

Clear expression

"The niftiest turn of phrase, the most elegant flight of rhetorical fancy, isn't worth beans next to a clear thought clearly expressed."

—⚬ JEFF GREENFIELD

When writing or speaking, we may get carried away with complicated words and sentence structure. It sounds sophisticated. But, is it all that sophisticated if a clear meaning was not communicated to the reader or listener? In successful communication, the goal is to transfer one of our thoughts into the mind of another. If our fancy words and terminology detract from that goal, they are worthless.

I will speak and write clearly when I'm trying to share thoughts with other people. I don't need to use complicated sentences to describe my ideas.

What works, what doesn't

"If it's working, keep doing it.
If it's not working, stop doing it.
If you don't know what to do, don't do anything."

—⌾ DR. MELVIN KONNER

That sounds too easy, but it's a good philosophy. When frustrated by something, this little serenity exercise helps: Take a sheet of paper and draw a line down the middle. On one side, write, "What works." On the other side, write, "What doesn't work." When we start our lists, it's amazing how much clarity comes just in writing our thoughts.

When I'm frustrated, I'll remember to take a deep breath and give the problem some thought. I will get back to the basics of what works and what doesn't work, then act accordingly.

Showing up

> "*Ask God's blessing on your work, but don't ask him to do it for you.*"
>
> — DAME FLORA ROBSON

We look to Providence for that extra spark we need for success, but to succeed, we still need to put in the effort. Like waiting for inspiration or happiness to arrive, a job well done still depends on our willingness to show up and take action. Work does not magically complete itself; we're responsible for our fair share of effort.

I can pray for guidance, blessing, and strength to complete my work, but I still need to put in the appropriate elbow grease.

Small deeds done

> *Small deeds done are better than great deeds planned.*
>
> — PETER MARSHALL

It's better to take a small step and complete it than to jot down a fabulous plan we might not be able to accomplish. Sometimes we sabotage ourselves by planning something so large and cumbersome there's no way we can carry it out. "I have some great ideas," we say. "I just never have the time to complete them."

Maybe it's time to try that big idea in a miniature form. Most great deeds start with smaller versions. Think of them as a training ground. When we take on a small deed we can accomplish, others realize we keep our word, and we increase our own self-confidence.

I don't need to make grandiose plans in order to do something worthwhile. I will try scaling things down to be more manageable, so I can do something well.

The body knows

"*Emotion always has its roots in the unconscious and manifests itself in the body.*"

—◦ IRENE CLAREMONT DE CASTILLEJO

Most of us have experienced times when the connection between subtle emotions and physical health became clear. When we're feeling our best about life, we notice that an achy joint no longer hurts, or we don't get sick even after being exposed to a mean cold. Similarly, we might feel a muscle we never noticed before tightening while we anticipate a stressful event.

"I didn't know it was affecting me that much," we say when we experience this tie between our feelings and bodies. It's important to listen to the signal our bodies are sending us.

Sometimes I'm not sure how I feel about things. I will pay attention to physical changes in my body to see if I can find a clue to my true feelings.

Acting on faith

"Faith . . . acts promptly and boldly on the occasion, on slender evidence."

—JOHN HENRY CARDINAL NEWMAN

It's comforting to choose a path that seems well-lit and predictable. But, once in a while, we seem to know with inexplicable confidence that it's time to take a risk. Moving in faith takes a joyful heart and a willingness to surrender perfectionism. Those leaps, both big and small, bring us to a new level of living, thinking, and loving.

I don't always need tangible proof to make a wise choice. Faith is the quiet knowing that guides me even when the facts are sketchy.

Practice attention

" *Choice of attention, to pay attention to this and ignore that, is to the inner life what choice of action is to the outer.* "

—⟡ W.H. AUDEN

We know that it takes discipline and outward practice to change a bad physical habit, whether it's biting our fingernails or smoking. Worrying, fretful thoughts, and being easily distracted can be bad habits, too. Altering these inner paths takes just as much dedication and proactivity as changing a physical habit.

Determining our focus is founded equally on choosing what to ignore and what to improve. This subtle inner shift is the beginning of living in peace.

There is one area in my life where I would like to have more focused attention. I can choose to guide my thoughts away from distractions and toward a clear focus.

Concentration

" *Concentration is everything. On the day I'm performing, I don't hear anything anyone says to me.* "

— LUCIANO PAVAROTTI

Tunnel vision sets in when we prepare to lead a group, perform in front of an audience, or begin an important conversation. No distraction can get through. The event or action becomes so vital that we don't sweat the small stuff.

We conserve and focus our energy. The only thing that matters is the moment we are in. It's difficult to live constantly in such a state of total focus; it is wonderful that we can draw it from within ourselves when we need it.

I have the ability to enter a state of pure, undistracted focus.

Take a deep breath

"The first rule is to keep an untroubled spirit. The second is to look things in the face and know them for what they are."

——&ographic; MARCUS AURELIUS

Too often, when we are troubled, we evaluate a situation and decide what our attitude and reaction ought to be. The circumstance determines our level of peace. The challenge looks stressful, so we feel stressed and then begin to think from a place of fear rather than creativity.

Finding a foundation of peace first, before evaluating, is a better approach. It's not denying the facts, it's simply deciding to operate from a place of internal security instead of letting the facts rattle us. Moving in that state of peace, we observe and assess, and then make our decisions with a clear mind.

I am safe. I am at peace. I recognize there will be many options for transforming a difficult situation into an opportunity.

Legacy of love

❝*Love is the only thing we can carry with us when we go, and it makes the end so easy.*❞

—◎ LOUISA MAY ALCOTT

When looking back from the end of a life stage or at the end of a lifetime, it is the remembrances of shared love that weave meaning into our journey.

Yes, love is the only thing we take with us, and our experiences together are our lasting legacy. The patterns of loving communication we set in motion are passed down for generations, through our children or mentoring relationships.

Every transition is easier if we know our legacy is founded in love.

I am finding new ways to express and receive love.

Intentional kindness

"Kindness in words creates confidence. Kindness in thinking creates profoundness. Kindness in giving creates love."

—— LAO TZU

Kindness often involves simple in-passing moments. It might be a patient smile, an encouraging comment, letting another person go first. At a greater depth, it involves well-thought-out words and actions toward the people in our family, or social and work circles.

Beginning in our thoughts about and attitudes toward others, kindness is a prism we look through that influences our responses to others. We step outside ourselves and see ways we can cultivate growth with others. We are ready when the opportunity presents itself.

I see how a small kindness can transform my relationships by making others feel better, thus changing the atmosphere among us.

Shared laughter

"A good laugh makes any interview, or any conversation, so much better."

—⌒ BARBARA WALTERS

A shared laugh ties people together. Laughing at a common experience, a mistake we empathize with, or a shared joy makes our foibles a little easier to deal with and doubles our moments of delight.

Laughter can make us vulnerable. When we laugh together, we set aside some of our formalities and connect in a way that acknowledges each other's humanity.

It isn't good to be serious all the time. I am free to laugh at myself, and even better, I am free to laugh with others at the awkward and silly moments we share.

Faith in others

"We must have infinite faith in each other."
—HENRY DAVID THOREAU

When we expect the best from others, we help make it possible for them to be, do, and create their best. We've heard the example of the child who is told she is bad or untrustworthy; she rapidly begins to fulfill that expectation. Conversely, when we give the same child a new responsibility, empower her to fulfill it, and then repeatedly affirm that we trust her to carry out the task, it is likely she will.

Parts of us remain childlike and responsive to others' expectations throughout our entire lives. It is an act of grace to have faith in the people around us, offering to hold open the door to their growth and transformation.

I have faith in others. I communicate that by telling them I believe in their abilities and trust them to keep their word.

Character starts small

"*We become just by performing just actions,
temperate by performing temperate actions,
brave by performing brave actions.*"

— ARISTOTLE

Strong character traits are like any part of
our physical body in that they become strong
through intentional, appropriate use. When we
find ourselves wishing we were better or more
accomplished in a certain quality, the best remedy is to practice a small action that embodies
that quality.

Starting with an easily accomplished task, we
find success and develop the momentum to try
again. Those small actions accumulate until they
are habits that flow like breathing.

I wish I had more of a certain characteristic. I will
take one small action to embody that quality.

The art of guessing

"Living is a form of not being sure, not knowing what next, or how. The moment you know how, you begin to die a little. The artist never entirely knows. We guess. We may be wrong, but we take leap after leap in the dark."

—⟋ AGNES DE MILLE

Whether our life work is in the arts, science, business, caregiving, law, politics, or any other field, we all face uncertainty. The artist's challenge of facing a blank canvas is common to us all.

What now? Will I make the right choice? What will my loved ones think? At some point, the questions and perfectionism are set aside, and we leap.

I like the feeling of certainty. I also recognize that I grow whenever I face uncertainty and find a way through it.

Nay-sayers

"Do not attempt to do a thing unless you are sure of yourself, but do not relinquish it simply because someone else is not sure of you."

—⁂ STEWART E. WHITE

It is healthy to take some time to evaluate a risk and decide if we're ready. Once we've decided to try our plan, it doesn't make sense to stop simply because someone else has doubts. There is no shortage of nay-sayers and people opposed to change. We can listen to and consider their concerns, but we must decide for ourselves if the risk is still a worthy one.

I will evaluate and consider my risks. I will listen to others' concerns. But, I will not let another's hesitancy become the sole hang-up that causes me to set aside a good idea.

Simple prayers

"The fewer the words, the better the prayer."

— MARTIN LUTHER

Whether for ourselves or for another, the purest prayers require few words. They are uncluttered expressions of the heart. God knows our needs before they are expressed. The purpose of prayer is not as an outlet for us to vent, but as a way to find connection. This requires few words.

I do not have to use many words to express and clarify myself to the Divine. Sometimes one word is enough.

Comfortable with ourselves

❝ *The worst loneliness is not to be comfortable with yourself.* ❞

—⌒ MARK TWAIN

To be alone is not necessarily to be lonely. We may feel lonely even within our relationships if we are not comfortable with ourselves. When we take time for solitude, we can grow in our ability to feel comfortable in our own skin. Like any skill, this takes practice.

Sometimes, when we're not happy with ourselves, we look to other people to fill our time and keep us entertained. There is rich contentment that comes from a self-accepting solitude. We take that contentment with us when we return to our relationships with others. It brightens and energizes all our interactions.

I will take time to practice solitude, to learn to be comfortable alone as well as in my relationships.

Recycle and re-use

"Make good use of bad rubbish."
— ELIZABETH BERESFORD

Recycling plastic, cans, paper, and glass is a common activity. It feels good to put some of our trash to good use. We can embrace a similar attitude toward experiences, interactions, and circumstances, too. Sometimes we feel like life has left us with a pile of junk. We wonder, "How am I going to get rid of all this?"

It's possible to regard the rubbish in our lives as raw material. It may be unusual raw material, but it's useful nonetheless. It is more productive to ask, "What can I create from these fragments? How can I assemble this into something fantastic?"

Whether I'm looking at a garage full of clutter or difficult memories in my past, I have some junk piles in my personal terrain. I wonder what I can make with these scraps or how I can re-use them in a creative way.

Practicing tolerance

> *Tolerance is the positive and cordial effort to understand another's beliefs, practices, and habits without necessarily sharing or accepting them.*
>
> —JOSHUA LOTH LIEBMAN

As we get to know people of different backgrounds and belief systems, we will find areas in which we have no common ground.

Though we may not agree with the other person, we recognize that they have their own story, upbringing, culture, and beliefs, just as we do. We can discuss and face our differences, but the differences don't need to prevent us from interacting again. In fact, having more interaction will increase our capacity to empathize while holding our own identity intact.

Some belief systems and cultures are mysterious to me. I will try conversing more with someone who is different from me, to further my understanding.

First and foremost, love

"I knew what my job was; it was to go out and meet the people and love them."

— DIANA, PRINCESS OF WALES

Virtually every spiritual tradition reminds us of this core purpose in life. We are simply to love others and grow in our capacity to express and fully communicate that love. In order to truly love another, we must heal ourselves and, as we gain strength, be willing to reach out and risk. Therein lies the heart and soul of a whole and meaningful life.

To live is to love. It really is that simple. I'll begin with myself and then allow my love to overflow toward others.

Appreciating nature

"Nature has been for me, for as long as I remember, a source of solace, inspiration, adventure, and delight; a home, a teacher, a companion."

—— LORRAINE ANDERSON

The natural environment is more than just dirt, trees, lakes, and mountains. When we slow down long enough to enjoy nature, we're rewarded with great lessons in peace, life cycles, design, and exploration. Nature has a presence and a personality all its own, inspiring us to relate to the sea or the wilderness as a dear friend. In the presence of nature, listen and remember we are an inseparable part of it.

Whether I live in a rural community or a crowded city, I can take time to appreciate the natural world—even if it's simply admiring the leaves of a tree outside my window. I am grateful for all the little miracles of the natural world.

Healthy relationships take work

> *"Human beings are born into this little span of life of which the best thing is its friendships and intimacies . . . and yet they leave their friendships and intimacies with no cultivation, to grow as they will by the roadside."*
>
> —⌘ WILLIAM JAMES

When we want to learn something new, we take a class. When we want to complete a project, we make time to work on it. When we want to see a change in our community, we get involved.

Similarly, it takes effort and attention to be a good friend or partner. Relationships do not grow and remain healthy on their own. If we value our relationships, we will cultivate them and make time for them.

My relationships are my most important commitment. I will live and schedule my time and energy to reflect this.

The most precious gift

"If a person gives you his time, he can give you no more precious gift."

—⌒ FRANK TYGER

Of all our resources, time is the most valuable. Unlike many material resources, once spent, time can never be recovered. When other people give us their time, we need to regard it as a precious gift. They are giving of themselves, spending a part of their lives with us.

We must not take it for granted. We can honor this gift by paying close attention to our friends while we are with them and by showing our gratitude.

When people give their time to me, I'll take it seriously. I will remember to thank them and offer to return the favor.

All our present blessings

"Gladly accept the gifts of the present hour."

—HORACE

What good things are happening at this very moment? What can we be grateful for right now? There are always blessings we can count. Our food, clothing, and shelter are just the beginning. We can be glad for good companions, for the nation we live in, for the education we have that enables us to read these words. The gifts of the moment are endless. As soon as we open our eyes to everything that's packed into this hour, we are filled with gratitude.

What do I have to be thankful for right now? I will think of this for a moment and let those gifts rest deep in my heart.

Birds of a feather

"Seek those who find your road agreeable, your personality and mind stimulating, your philosophy acceptable, and your experiences helpful. Let those who do not, seek their own kind."

—JEAN-HENRI FABRE

Occasionally we get stuck hoping to impress someone who simply isn't into our passions and ideas. Instead of trying to persuade them to embrace our perspective, or pressuring ourselves to be someone we're not, maybe we need to quit trying to fit a square peg in a round hole. There are plenty of people in the world with whom we can make friends, whether close or casual. We can let go of those who aren't interested in connecting with us and find others who are.

I welcome differing opinions and personalities in my social group, but, if someone simply doesn't want to connect with me, I won't try to force it.

Exceeding expectations

"I've always tried to go a step past wherever people expected me to end up."

— BEVERLY SILLS

It is a unique delight to exceed others' expectations of us. In work and in play, it's fun to show off a little now and again. Breaking the status quo and rising above what was required, we bring fresh energy and enthusiasm to a situation. Ultimately, we are only competing with ourselves and growing our own sense of personal best.

There are areas in my life where I compromise and settle for the norm. I will bring some fresh energy into those areas by exceeding the basic expectations.

Listening prayer

"*In prayer, more is accomplished by listening than by talking.*"

—⤜ JANE FRANCES DE CHANTAL

Prayer is like any other conversation. We glean much more by quieting ourselves, asking questions, and listening close for the reply. What a challenge it can be to simply listen! We want so much to add our own commentary.

There is so much chatter and noise in our lives and in our minds. Deep prayer involves turning the volume down on that chatter. In the silence, finally, we can begin to hear the small, still voice of wisdom.

As I lie down to rest, my body relaxes. I will rest my mind as well. In that quiet state, instead of grasping for the next thought I would like to express in prayer, I will continue in stillness and listen for wisdom's voice.

Receiving forgiveness

"*Many promising reconciliations have broken down because while both parties came prepared to forgive, neither party came prepared to be forgiven.*"

—CHARLES WILLIAM

It takes grace to forgive another person, and it takes a special measure of grace to receive forgiveness. Sometimes it's a relief to know the other forgives us, but sometimes it feels awkward. Maybe it's because being forgiven requires that we admit we did something wrong, and might need to change.

I can have the grace not only to give forgiveness, but also to receive it.

We are unique

"Nobody can be exactly like me. Sometimes even I have trouble doing it."

—◇ TALLULAH BANKHEAD

We are all unique. Just as there is always something new to learn about our friends, there is also something new we can learn about ourselves each day. Sometimes we find parts of our lives where we seem to be trying to be someone else. It is a creative challenge to uncover the core of who we really are and then change in ways that are truer to ourselves.

I am unique. I enjoy discovering more about my own gifts and interests and choose to develop those areas in a way that is true to myself.

Awakened strength

"A single event can awaken within us a stranger totally unknown to us."

—A NTOINE DE S AINT-E XUPÉRY

It might happen when we show a new flash of healthy assertiveness during a conflict with someone who is refusing to hear our position. We might surprise ourselves when we stop to play baseball with a friend's child, and then discover we would like to teach. When a loved one has cancer, we take a leadership role, organizing a citywide fundraiser.

The possible catalysts can be anything. We are left marveling, "I didn't know I had it in me to do that!"

I wonder what strengths lie within me that I have never expressed. I welcome the circumstances and inspirations that will spark the change.

Be the change

> "*Sometimes you gotta create what you want to be a part of.*"
>
> —⟋ GERI WEITZMAN

We might wish our neighborhood had a nicer park, or that our workplace was more efficient. We might wish our town offered more community education, or think it would be great if our civic club would do a charity fundraiser. Sometimes, we are the ones who need to bring our ideas to life.

Grassroots initiatives work that way. They start, grow, and mature from the ground up, beginning with people like us who have a great idea and choose to take a first step.

I have some great ideas. Instead of sitting and wishing, I'm going to decide on small ways to bring my ideas to life. Then, I'll do them.

Response instead of reaction

"A life of reaction is a life of slavery, intellectually and spiritually. One must fight for a life of action, not reaction."

—⟡ RITA MAE BROWN

Reactions are directed and even controlled by the other person or circumstance. Life in reaction mode leaves us feeling shaky and over-whelmed. We're not sure who we are anymore because we're not making our own choices—someone or something else has control.

Coming back to ourselves, we remember the importance of healthy response. We're acting out of our own values and sense of mission once again. There will always be surprises in life, but we can calmly respond in light of our strengths and sense of security.

I will respond rather than react. Whenever I feel myself getting reactive, I will take the time I need to come back to an attitude of calm, thoughtful response.

True success

"When all is said and done, success without happiness is the worst kind of failure."

— LOUIS BINSTOCK

Especially with financial, career, and athletic success, the work can take so much time and effort, and the goal can become so consuming, that we lose our original joy. Perhaps we wind up sacrificing the little pleasures and time spent with loved ones in order to "make it."

Making it to the top of the ladder doesn't feel good if we are burned out when we get there. It's important to make time along the way to feed our souls, delight in friendship, and laugh at ourselves. It may take longer to get to our summit, but we will get there with the personal energy and relationships to really enjoy it.

No goal is so important that I must forfeit my sanity and joy to achieve it. I choose to make time for happiness all along the way.

Good health is everything

"*He who has health, has hope; and he who has hope, has everything.*"

—⌒ ARABIAN PROVERB

Our health is precious. We don't know how precious until it's taken away. We and our loved ones know the pain of poor health, whether it's a bad cold or an extended illness. It's hard to make any decisions or do any of the things that energize us. Sickness is discouraging.

How fantastic it feels when health is restored! With good health comes creativity, ability, and hope—all we need to make our way along even the most difficult journey.

I will take some time to breathe deep and think of how thankful I am for my good health. If I'm not feeling well today, I will remember healthier times and look forward to better days.

Bad, good, or best

> "Life is a series of choices between the bad, the good, and the best. Everything depends on how we choose."
>
> —⌒ VANCE HAVNER

Making mindful choices can be a chore. It's easy to make a choice based on what we've always done, or what seems the easiest or most comfortable. But is it best? It can be a challenge to face that question head-on and wrestle with the follow-through and dedication it might require of us.

I want to be more aware in my decisions. I will avoid unhealthy options, but more than that, I want to create a lifestyle of following the best path. It might include choices that require more time, effort, and care. It will be worth it.

Actions tell all

> ❝*Trust only movement. Life happens at the level of events, not of words. Trust movement.*
>
> —⌁ ALFRED ADLER

With loved ones, at work, and in world events, it's true that talk can be cheap. People may tell us who they wish they were, or what they hope to do someday, but we learn an individual's character through how he or she acts. That takes time and observation.

Eventually, we begin to discern on what levels we can actually trust people. We learn they have a track record for carrying out, or not carrying out, commitments. That is what we wind up trusting, regardless of spoken words.

I will watch people's actions to discern their character. What they do is a truer expression of their level of integrity than their words.

Step into the water

"If your ship doesn't come in, swim out to it."
—☙ JONATHAN WINTERS

Successful people seem to have a knack for making their own opportunities or getting closer to opportunities they've heard about. If we sit and wait for success to suddenly materialize, there is a chance it will spontaneously happen—but it's a slim chance, indeed! When we have a dream, there is only one way to see it through: Set a course and then begin taking a few small steps into the water.

The next time I hear myself talking about luck or chance, I'll think of a way I can better the odds of achieving my goal, and then take a small step in the right direction.

Sharing your time

❝ *Time isn't a commodity, something you pass around like cake. Time is the substance of life. When anyone asks you to give your time, they're really asking for a chunk of your life.* ❞

—⟶ ANTOINETTE BOSCO

Our time is priceless. It cannot be returned, but it can be beautifully rewarded. When people ask for our time, we want to know that it's appreciated. Sometimes people demand our time as if it's their right. It's okay for us to speak up and say, "No, I can't do that," or, "I can help with that, but not today." As the saying goes, "Poor planning on your part does not necessitate an emergency on my part." We are free to scrutinize and decide whether or not we want to spend our time in a certain fashion. Then, when we do share our time, it is a conscious gift.

When I give my time to another person, I am giving myself to them. I am happy to share, but I will also be careful that others are not taking advantage of me.

Too much close contact

"*The chain of friendship, however bright, does not stand the attrition of constant close contact.*"

— Sir Walter Scott

We are happy when we're with our friends. We want to spend more time with them and lament how much time we've been apart. But, it's also healthy for close friends to spend time away from each other. Whether it's best friends, roommates or spouses, we all need to be apart once in a while.

Being together all the time hangs too many needs and expectations on a relationship. We can grate on each other. When we're apart, we find other ways to meet our needs, recover our identity as individuals, and come back with fresh stories and energy from our separate experiences.

Because my closest friends are important to me, I will spend some healthy time apart from them.

Prayer as a personal barometer

"*Prayer at its best is the expression of the total life, for all things else being equal, our prayers are only as powerful as our lives.*"

—A.W. Tozer

We pray out of the overflow of the heart. What is deep inside us and how do we value our own spirituality? The nature of our prayers gives an honest assessment. Do we only pray for our own welfare, for things we want, or out of sheer desperation? Do we pray as an act of conversation? Our core beliefs about life and God bubble up in our prayers. As we mature in understanding and create a healthy life, the tone and timbre of our prayers also changes.

I will pay attention to how and when I pray. There can be clues regarding areas in my life where I might like to grow more.

Sleep well and stay healthy

"Health is the first muse, and sleep is the condition to produce it."

— RALPH WALDO EMERSON

Sleep is no trivial luxury. It is a physical need like air and food. We occasionally cheat our bodies of sleep in order to finish a project or enjoy the company of friends, but we must not make a habit of it. Sleep-deprivation is hard on the immune system, and makes it hard to think clearly.

During the most stressful times, when we need good health and all our troubleshooting skills and creativity intact, we may find ourselves missing sleep. That is precisely the time we need it most.

Getting enough sleep is a serious part of keeping myself healthy. I'll keep a set bedtime that permits me enough sleep to feel well rested when I wake.

Children are messy

> "My father used to play with my brother and me in the yard. Mother would come out and say, 'You're tearing up the grass.' 'We're not raising grass,' Dad would reply. 'We're raising boys.'"
>
> — HARMON KILLEBREW

We might be playing with our own kids, nieces and nephews, or friends' children, but one thing holds constant: Kids are messy. There is no way around it. If we want a perfectly tidy home, we must hang a "No Kids" sign on the door. No matter what, we wouldn't do that!

When we welcome children into our lives, we accept the mess that comes with them. We can even delight in it with them. When they are older, we'll wonder at how fast they grew and how quickly they left behind the days of finger-paint, piles of blocks, and torn-up grass.

I enjoy the children in my life. It is a privilege to help them learn about the world and to join them in play. I won't waste time fretting over any mess they make.

Adventurous spirit

"I feel very adventurous. There are so many doors to be opened, and I'm not afraid to look behind them."

—◯ ELIZABETH TAYLOR

Let's go! We were always ready for an adventure as kids; nothing could hold us back from exploring our world. We can recapture that enthusiasm. There is much to explore where we live right now. It can help to take the perspective of a tourist for a day, to pretend we are only passing through the places that are so familiar to us.

With fresh eyes, we ask questions we haven't asked before. Choosing to notice the intriguing details of our surroundings, we carry that attitude into our work and relationships, too. An ordinary life is suddenly trembling with possibility.

I like to walk through life with an adventurous spirit. There are doors of possibility all around me.

Synchronicity

"Whenever we have the chutzpah to take the first risky step toward a defined and passionate goal, our path suddenly lines itself with opportunities, resources, and helping hands."

—ANNA BJÖRKLUND

Every opportunity for growth and change involves equal parts elbow grease and luck. It seems as soon as we make the choice to put some effort and personal risk into achieving a dream, other factors arrange themselves accordingly.

The week we decide to take a class to learn a new hobby, we wind up having a conversation with someone who is skilled at that craft and would love to share some tips. The day we decide to start a business, we get a call from a relative who knows a great potential client.

I know I need to put in a lot of effort to achieve my goals. It's encouraging to know there will be plenty of help along the way.

Love lightens the burden

"I see their souls, and I hold them in my hands, and because I love them they weigh nothing."

—⎰ PEARL BAILEY

We can be guarded when caring for others and helping them with their problems. What if their issues drain us? What if they take up a lot of time? When we reach out to others in compassion, we discover that the reaching out creates its own energy. Love provides its own time and resources. The others' burdens do not weigh us down when we let love carry the load.

I won't be afraid of having compassion for others. I trust that love will fuel my actions.

A few sweet words

> *"Sweet words are like honey, a little may refresh,
> but too much gluts the stomach."*
> — ANNE BRADSTREET

Sometimes when talking sweetly with loved ones, we're tempted to phrase things several ways to make sure our point is understood. But "less is more" in intimate conversation. Kind speech is more powerful and memorable when we distill it and present it like a rare and precious gem. Unique and powerful, the words stand out. Excess only negates itself, leaving the other feeling embarrassed or questioning our sincerity.

When I have something sweet to say, I will think it through and boil it down to the most important sentiment. I'll let my loved ones savor the moment rather than overwhelming them with my eloquence.

Release and grow in love

"In hatred as in love, we grow like the thing we brood upon. What we loathe, we graft into our very soul."

—☙ MARY RENAULT

We've seen people consumed by hate. They felt enraged, and then stayed there, continuing to despise the one who hurt them. That's where the story turns tragic. Now the hurt one continues in self-destructive bitterness.

We must not get caught in that rut. The object of our hate becomes ingrained in our identity; we become what we focus on. The answer is to practice forgiveness. It's only when we release the other completely that we are free to become ourselves again.

If hatred flares up in my heart, I will take it seriously. It's damaging. I'll spend time in prayer or meditation and work on forgiveness to bring myself back to a more positive focus.

Contentment greater than riches

" If thou covetest riches, ask not but for contentment, which is an immense treasure. "

— SA'DI

There is always a greater amount we could wish for. When our debts our paid, we want more money in savings; when we have an emergency fund, we wish to invest; when our investments clipping along, we want more so we can care for family.

Yet, even a person who lives in a humble dwelling with only enough food for a few days might be viewed as comfortable by someone who has no home. Our sense of wealth is relative. When we are content, our eyes open wider to appreciate all that we have, no matter what our current station in life.

If I focus on growing my sense of gratitude and contentment, I will feel wealthy no matter what I have or don't have.

Whole-hearted help

> *"Never reach out your hand unless you're willing to extend an arm."*
>
> —⌒ ELIZABETH FULLER

Token helpfulness isn't often appreciated. We see the problem, we want to help, but we don't really want to commit too much to it—and then we stop short of actually doing anything. Those involved wonder why we even bothered. Did we really care?

If we wish to help, we must give it some thought and decide on a specific way we can make a difference. Time is short and finances may be limited, but if we want to get involved, it is best if we have a clear intention.

If I'm going to help someone, I'll do it wholeheartedly. Whether I give my time, a donation, or provide a listening ear, I'll be completely present and expect that I may need to follow up afterwards, too.

Affecting the next generation

> *"What is buried in the past of one generation falls to the next to claim."*

— Susan Griffin

There are many things we'd rather forget than explain to the next generation. Our hidden flaws, wrongdoings, and secrets have a way of simmering to the surface for the next generation to deal with. Evading the hard issues only ensures that future generations will have more unanswered questions after we are gone. They will be better equipped if we give them the details now. Admitting our responsibility gives us a chance to heal and build our relationships with the next generation.

Whether I have children or not, I have relationships with younger people. I will make sure I clearly talk to them about the choices I've made that may affect them. I want to build a bridge between our generations.

Just being honest

_"Honesty without compassion and understanding
is not honesty, but subtle hostility."_

— ROSE N. FRANZBLAU

"Well, I was just being honest," we mutter when
someone seems hurt by a harsh observation
we make. Honesty is the best policy, but we
shouldn't use that as a cop-out to justify acting
mean-spirited. If we have difficult words to
speak, we need to do it in a way that honors
and respects another person's feelings. If we
don't have time for that, we certainly don't have
time for cleaning up after the offense we're
about to cause!

When I want to be honest about a sticky issue, I
will look closely at my motives. Do I really want
to help the other person, or am I using this as an
opportunity to hurt them? I'll wait until I have a
constructive attitude and can speak with
genuine concern.

Teach a person to fish

"The greatest good you can do for another is not just to share your riches, but to reveal to him his own."

—⌒ BENJAMIN DISRAELI

When we only give of our resources, we tend to create dependency. The other person is grateful, but might still have trouble getting on his or her own feet. Through mentorship and creative questioning, we can help that person discover their own strengths, talents, and possibilities.

Initially, this takes more time than simply tossing money at the problem. In the long run, our protégé grows more confident and no longer needs our help. In fact, they might mentor others in turn. Our investment of time and teaching will grow exponentially.

My financial donations are good and helpful, but before I choose to donate money, I will consider whether there is a way I can affect the same issue through mentoring someone one-to-one.

Gossip is unproductive

"Gossip speaks volumes of the character of its speaker."

—✦ ANNA BJÖRKLUND

When we hear someone gossip, we begin to wonder more about the one who's gossiping than the one who is the subject of the gossip. Is any of this true? Is this person trustworthy? Will they turn around and gossip about me, too? We become guarded around them, careful never to discuss anything about ourselves that might make us vulnerable.

Gossip isn't productive. In our families, social circles, and workplaces, we can call gossip what it is and ask the speaker to stop. A simple "I don't want to talk about this," usually does the trick.

I will avoid gossiping. I will speak up if it seems like a conversation is turning into gossip.

Love must be shared

"For we must share, if we would keep,
that blessing from above;
Ceasing to give, we cease to have;
such is the law of love."

—◦ RICHARD C. TRENCH

How can it be that the most cheerful and energetic people are also the ones who give of themselves the most? In all its expressions—friendship, family, romance—love takes energy and work, but somehow magically feeds that back to us as well.

The "return" might not be from the same person we just gave to. In the economy of love, when we are miserly and guarded, we stay small. When we give of the little we have, suddenly a greater measure is given to us.

I will be abundant in expressing my love for others.

Spiritual acts of kindness

> *To give pleasure to a single heart by a single kind act is better than a thousand head-bowings in prayer.*
>
> — SA'DI

Most spiritual traditions acknowledge that we can follow every rule and practice every ritual, but our religious observance is empty if we do not care for our fellow humans. At the center of healthy faith is a desire to grow in love. That is our purpose. When we do something thoughtful, solely to please the other and with no concern about whether we will get something back, we touch the heart of the Divine.

In my busy days, I will not forget my true purpose: to practice love and connection with those around me.

Soon-to-be adult

"*A child is a temporarily disabled and stunted
version of a larger person, whom you will
someday know. Your job is to help them overcome
the disabilities associated with their size and
inexperience so that they get on with being that
larger person.*"

—◌ BARBARA EHRENREICH

The children in our lives need us to guide and
equip them. Thinking of them as soon-to-be
adults rather than just kids can remind us to
treat them with respect. The most important
thing we can do is help them grow their interests, talents, and beliefs. We need to show them
not only how to survive, but how to thrive. This
is what helps them mature—and rewards us
with good friends.

I will treat the children in my life with respect. I
can help them learn about their world and
about themselves.

Worthy of our help?

> " People who won't help others in trouble 'because they got into trouble through their own fault' would probably not throw a lifeline to a drowning man until they learned whether he fell in through his own fault or not. "

—⁜ SYDNEY J. HARRIS

Do we really want to help our neighbor? Didn't they get into that mess because of their own choices? It's odd how often we judge others as "not qualified" to receive our help.

What if *we* were in trouble? That day will come. Most of the trouble we've had in our lives has come, to some extent, from our own actions. Yet, there were people who helped us anyway. The fact that they would help us, whether or not we were responsible for at least part of the problem, spurred us to change and grow.

I won't get hung up wondering if someone is worthy of my assistance. I'll simply look for an appropriate way to help and then do so, no strings attached.

When it's good to quit

> *Everyone should keep a mental wastepaper basket and the older he grows the more things he will consign to it—torn up to irrecoverable tatters.*
>
> —⌾ SAMUEL BUTLER

If at first we don't succeed, try and try again. And, if at some point we determine the idea is flagrantly flawed, we should toss it out. It's good to persist in a pursuit, but it takes even more wisdom to know when to quit. Quitting is not always about giving up. It can be about honestly recognizing that something is simply not going to work. Scrap the idea. Move on to something else.

When I'm trying to make a certain concept work, it's okay for me to decide to quit. I can tell whether it requires more perseverance or is simply a bad idea.

Love forgives

"*Forgiveness is the most tender part of love.*"
—☙ JOHN SHEFFIELD

Love has so many tender aspects. Its kind
words, touches, and generosities abound.
But forgiveness is the most impressive. At
the moment we consider trying to get even
or retreat with hurt feelings, we can instead
approach with a surprising softness. It is that
quality that makes love last.

As I grow my capacity to love, I grow my ability to
give and receive forgiveness.

Mundane tasks

"Every job has drudgery . . . The first secret of happiness is the recognition of this fundamental fact."

—◊ M.C. McIntosh

Once in a while, work is just work. There are repetitive chores we need to do every day; there are housekeeping tasks, paperwork, and reports to file. We don't enjoy every aspect of our role, but on the whole, it's a good option for us right now. It's important to be able to discern whether the position is a poor fit, or simply has a few mundane aspects—just like any job.

I will take an honest look at my job right now and decide whether it's not working for me, or if I'm just tired of a few difficult tasks. Any job I take on will have moments when I feel I need to grin and bear it.

Facing fear of the unknown

"Anything I've ever done that ultimately was worthwhile . . . initially scared me to death."

—⟶ BETTY BENDER

It's scary when the stakes are high. The unknown is a big question mark, and we're wired to preserve our safety. It can be hard to tell if it's our truest instincts that are telling us to back away—in which case, we should listen—or if it's just a garden-variety fear.

When it's just plain fear of the unknown, it's good to stretch ourselves. How many times have we been afraid to try something new, and then felt so grateful later that we took courage and did it anyway? Whether we're making a big positive change or taking a risk in a relationship, it's normal to be nervous. Reminding ourselves that it will be worthwhile, we take a step and do it. Each new success makes us a little braver.

I've taken risks in the past that opened the door to new chapters in my life. It was definitely worth it. I can be courageous like that again.

Pray and take action

Trust in Allah, but tie your camel.

—◌ ARABIAN PROVERB

We can lift all our concerns in prayer and release them to our higher power. It brings peace to know there are forces outside ourselves at work on our behalf. We're not alone. We must not let that become an excuse for irresponsibility or laziness, however. We are still active in our own lives and accountable for our own actions and omissions.

I will release my concerns in prayer while calmly taking action wherever I can. That's the heart of serenity.

Accepting a friend's flaws

"Two persons cannot long be friends if they cannot forgive each other's little failings."

—JEAN DE LA BRUYÈRE

People are not perfect. Yet, from time to time, we expect our friends to be. Can we still be friends after we discover their flaws? Can they be friends with us after they see ours? Casual acquaintances and workmates can keep up a shiny front for each other. Close friendship requires equal parts of vulnerability and acceptance.

I know my friends are not perfect, but neither am I. We can accept each other, flaws and all.

Spare moments

"Guard well your spare moments. They are like uncut diamonds. Discard them and their value will never be known. Improve them and they will become the brightest gems in a useful life."

—⟡ RALPH WALDO EMERSON

The quiet time before the household wakes. A coffee break. Waiting for a bus. Arriving at a meeting early. Relaxing after dinner. How do we spend our down time? Improving our spare moments does not necessarily mean letting them fill with stressful to-do list tasks. Increasing their value begins by asking what we really need right now. Perhaps it's meditation, conversation, literature, solitude, laughter, or creativity. We can intentionally season our lives with meaningful spare moments.

My spare moments are precious. I will set aside one break each day for something that enriches my soul.

Physical limits

"Our own physical body possesses a wisdom which we who inhabit the body lack. We give it orders which make no sense."

—⌀ HENRY MILLER

Sometimes the requests we make of our bodies go over and above the call of duty and outside the realm of healthy discipline. Missing sleep, eating poorly, sitting at an unhealthy work station, rarely exercising, or lifting something that is too heavy—all can result in bad health or injury.

The body's desires are fairly straightforward: nourishment, shelter, self-care, rest, and movement. It's not surprising that those elements make for a balanced life for the soul, too.

When I honor and respect what my body needs to stay healthy, I find myself living a life that is healthier for my soul and mind as well. I will be more alert to my physical needs.

A time to work

66*Talk doesn't cook rice.*99

——☙ CHINESE PROVERB

There's a time for dreaming, brainstorming, and discussing possibilities, but ideas only come to fruition if we begin to work on them. While letting our creativity grow and thrive, we also need to keep track of our basic daily needs.

We can balance all our needs. Creativity and pragmatism, socialization and work, play and structure. What matters is being able to see the right moment and timing for each. There's a time to talk about plans, and there's a time to quit talking and begin to work.

It's good to be practical. To have a balanced life, I need to recognize when it's time to settle into a task and work until it's done.

Never outgrow love

"A baby is born with a need to be loved—and never outgrows it."

—⌘ FRANK A. CLARK

We were made to love and be loved. It is a deep and essential need. Yet, sometimes, we speak with scorn about people who appear emotionally needy. They seem immature. Aren't there areas where we are vulnerable and needy, too? Is maturity really a measure of our ability to hide our needs?

With open eyes and a sense of humor, we can find appropriate ways to receive and give more love. We begin with loving ourselves and grow from there, discovering we can love others with our own boundaries intact.

I'll never outgrow my need for love, and I recognize and respect that those around me need love, too.

Everything will get done

"*Nature does not hurry, yet everything is accomplished.*"

—⸎ LAO TZU

Plants germinate, grow, and yield in response to the seasons. Animals raise their young and store up for the winter based on instinct. Other organisms undergo moments of stress, but, typically, it isn't the sustained stress that we humans are so adept at creating.

We're aware of the seasons and we have instincts along with strong intellect. Too often, however, we let our intellect override our senses. Our deadlines are artificial, yet they command our state of mind. We can take a cue from nature and slow down to a healthier pace.

When life gets too busy, instead of adding to the rush, I will take a deep breath and remember that everything will get done.

Self-sufficient happiness

"Happiness belongs to those who are sufficient unto themselves. For all external sources of happiness and pleasure are, by their very nature, highly uncertain, precarious, ephemeral, and subject to chance."

— ARTHUR SCHOPENHAUER

We are all interdependent; our friendships and interactions are precious and can be sources of great joy. But, we cannot depend so much on others that we need them to make us happy. The happiest people simmer with gladness regardless of whether they are in happy circumstances. A healthy self-sufficiency is the first step in developing an unshakeable sense of joy.

Sometimes I feel happy because of a conversation, event, or enjoyable activity. I don't have to rely only on those sources of happiness, however. I can find happiness within myself.

Blaming others

> "When you blame others, you give up your power to change."
>
> — ANONYMOUS

It hurts to shoulder the blame when we mess up, but it's vital to do so, especially if it's a bad habit or a mistake we've made several times. Denying or minimizing our part in it, or blaming others for our actions, only seem like safe and comfortable options.

"I only did it because he told me that …" Sentences with that tone end with the conclusion we did nothing wrong and, consequently, don't need to learn or grow. Blaming and denying keep us stagnant. We can only change if we admit it was our fault we missed the mark.

If I'm blaming others, I'm not likely to make any personal changes for the better. I will admit my mistakes and change my actions appropriately.

A simple manner of life

> *"I believe that a simple and unassuming manner of life is best for everyone, best both for the body and the mind."*
>
> —☙ ALBERT EINSTEIN

Good food, a warm home, trustworthy friends, and satisfying work. When all is said and done, we are simple creatures with a basic list of needs. We tend to expand that list though, creating needless complications. Our toys need repair and maintenance, our lifestyles require overtime hours, neglected bodies need extra medical care.

When we hit the pause button on our pace, we discover the pleasures of a home-cooked meal or a walk through the woods with a friend. Then we realize those unassuming activities were better for us all along.

Things don't have to be complicated or pretentious. I will look for ways to simplify my life.

Eloquence is concise

"True eloquence consists of saying all that should be said, and that only."

—François de La
Rochefoucauld

There are many situations in which we are tempted to fill the airwaves with words. We wonder, "Did they really understand me the first time? Will they get it with such a short explanation? Will they recognize my expertise if I take longer on my presentation?"

Our instinct is to talk more about the matter, to display words as if they were trophies or industry credentials. That's not usually necessary. Whether at work or in our private life, the most impressive communications are simple and concise. We don't need to embellish. In fact, others prefer that we don't.

I will speak and express myself with a concise, self-controlled eloquence. I don't need to expound excessively or add any sidebars to my main point.

Regretting wasted time

> *"Regret for time wasted can become a power for good in the time that remains, if we will only stop the waste and the idle, useless regretting."*
>
> —⟜ ARTHUR BRISBANE

If a marathon runner stumbles, it would make no sense if that runner stopped mid-race to lament about the sadness of stumbling and the damage it's done to their race time. We hope the runner, if suffering no injury, will recover quickly from the stumble and carry on, perhaps paying closer attention to their stride.

Regretting wasted time is itself a waste of time. When we find we have wasted our time, the best thing we can do is quickly face the lost moment, decide how to avoid that situation in the future, and keep going.

I know I have occasionally wasted my time. That's okay. I don't have to wallow in that loss. I can just learn from the mistake and plan my time more wisely.

Amusing our friends

"We cherish our friends not for their ability to amuse us, but for ours to amuse them."

—᧏ EVELYN WAUGH

It's great fun when a friend does or says something hilarious, but it's even more satisfying when we do something that sparks their sweet laughter. We love to see the gleam in their eyes—and to know we put it there. Lifting their spirits is a boost to our own.

I enjoy being able to cheer others up and make them laugh. I will look for opportunities to bring more laughter into my friendships.

Skip the cleaning

" The darn trouble with cleaning the house is it gets dirty the next day anyway, so skip a week if you have to. The children are the most important thing. "

—◌ BARBARA BUSH

Ultimately, care for the appearance of our home and all our other little daily chores need to be secondary to our relationships. Living and enjoying life are inherently messy. Where there is joy and play, there is movement, use—and crumbs. It's okay to leave some of it overnight, or even let it go for a week if it means we get to spend a little more time enjoying what really matters.

It's good to keep a clean house, but not at the expense of those I love. There are times when it's just fine for me to let the chores go and have some fun instead.

Live wholeheartedly

"*One day, with life and heart, is more than time enough to find a world.*"

—James Russell Lowell

If we go into each day with an attitude of exploration and expectancy, we will notice wonders that we glossed over yesterday. The world is shimmering with wonderful experiences, opportunities, and ideas. We just need to open our eyes and our hands to receive.

I've had times when my senses have been particularly alert, when I embraced life with my whole heart. When I wake tomorrow, I will choose that attitude of wonder. Who knows what I will discover?

Apologize, learn, and move on

> "*If you have behaved badly, repent, make what amends you can and address yourself to the task of behaving better next time.*"
>
> —᠔ ALDOUS HUXLEY

No one likes to hear a lot of excuses for bad behavior. Whether it's a foolish mistake or a flash of revenge on our part, we need to own it. It's time for an apology and whatever amends are appropriate. Then, as best as we can, we need to move along with a better attitude. It's unproductive to brood over the matter or to repeatedly revisit the offense with the person we've hurt. That only keeps all of us from moving on and learning.

When I make a mistake or hurt someone, I need to be quick to admit my wrongdoing and forthright in my apology. I need not torture myself over the matter. A single apology paired with a commitment to change is enough.

Influencing strong people

> "*It is easier to influence strong than weak characters in life.*"
>
> —⊱ MARGOT ASQUITH

Strong-willed people can seem intimidating—but we certainly know where they stand. For that reason, it can be more satisfying to persuade strong-willed people to our way of thinking. If they listen to us and decide we have a solid idea, they will not waver once they agree with us and will make a real commitment. People who tend to waffle can be hard to influence. We're never completely certain whether they agree with us—and they aren't sure, either!

I don't need to be intimidated when trying to persuade someone who holds strong opinions. I can be glad that they may soon agree to my opinion with the same tenacity.

Keep a light pack

"We can easily manage if we will only take each day, the burden appointed to it. But the load will be too heavy for us if we carry yesterday's burden over again today, and then add the burden of the morrow before we are required to bear it."

—JOHN NEWTON

Everything adds up. Stresses compound, worries about the future weigh us down. Soon we have a full backpack of regrets and what-ifs. It's so unnecessary.

What matters, all that matters, is this day. This day is where we may act, speak, and effect change. May we cover the rest with grace and laughter.

I don't need to keep picking up old burdens. Today is all I need to be concerned about. I'll have a more focused mind for handling tomorrow's challenges if I haven't tired myself worrying about them today.

Infinite possibility

> *"I thank You God for this most amazing day; for the leaping greenly spirits of trees and a blue true dream of sky; and for everything which is natural which is infinite which is yes."*
>
> — E.E. CUMMINGS

There is so much beauty in the natural world. It renews us and lifts our spirits whenever we give ourselves a moment to experience nature with all our senses alert. We remember how we are only a small part of this amazing place. We think of our planet in the context of the universe and feel humble.

Considering the infinite, our problems seem small, and we are more aware of all that is possible.

When I think of the size of the earth and the wonder of the natural world, it brings my life back down to an appropriate scale. I can feel thankful and present again.

Moments of being

> " *This—this was what made life: a moment of quiet*
> *the water falling in the fountain, the girl's voice . .*
> *a moment of captured beauty. He who is truly wis*
> *will never permit such moments to escape.* "
>
> —⌒ LOUIS L'AMOUR

Once in a while, we have one of those rare
"moments of being" when we are acutely aware
and appreciative of what we are experiencing.
We see or hear a common occurrence, but our
mind is suddenly attuned to the miracle of it all

It often happens when our spiritual eyes are
open wide for another reason. Perhaps we're
going through a major transition, struggling
with an illness, traveling far from home, or
wrestling with our sense of identity. Sometimes
the moment seems to come for no reason.
Regardless, it is precious.

I am thankful for those times when I'm suddenly
deeply present and aware of life. I will welcome
the moments, treasuring them and letting them
linger for a while.

266

Peeking out of our shell

> "Behold the turtle. He makes progress only when he sticks his neck out."
>
> —JAMES BRYANT CONANT

It's comfortable and safe in our little shell. That shell might be a routine, a job, a relationship, a habit. Whatever it is, it feels warm and familiar. Then comes the moment when we grow restless. It's been good, but we're ready to grow—to go! Like a turtle coming out of hiding, we peek out the door and look around. We stretch our legs and take a single step.

The risk is worth it. I will stick my head out of my shell once in a while to see if I'd like to go somewhere else.

Meaningful habits

"It is not in novelty but in habit that we find the greatest pleasure."

—⌒ RAYMOND RADIGUET

When we remember a chapter in our life during which we were especially satisfied, it's often not any grand event that stands out. Instead, we may recall a habit or routine that was particularly renewing and meaningful.

Perhaps it was that period when we visited the library every Thursday. Maybe it was while we had a job that allowed us to work from home two days each week. Or was it during that extended vacation when we took a long walk every day? These are the things that feed the soul on a daily basis. The pleasure they bring is lasting.

There are some healthy habits in my life right now. I am thankful for the way these simple practices enrich my life.

Too small for prayer

"Any concern too small to be turned into a prayer is too small to be made into a burden."

— CORRIE TEN BOOM

We vent a frustration to friends and they encourage us to pray or meditate about the matter. "Oh, it's not that big a deal," we mutter. Our complaint was, itself, a sideways act of prayer. Apparently, whatever it is, it's important to us. Why not transform it into an intentional act of prayer? Taking it seriously, taking ourselves seriously, we dedicate some time to prayer or meditation. In that space, we discover peace and let go of worry. The burden lifts.

If I am concerned enough to worry about something, I will meditate or pray.

Gentle critique

"Do not remove a fly from your friend's forehead with a hatchet."

—⌒ CHINESE PROVERB

Once we've been friends with someone for a while, their little idiosyncrasies and flaws become more obvious. What seems so clear to us doesn't even seem to be on the radar for them. Don't they realize how silly, bull-headed, or irrational they're acting? Much as it's tempting to be brusque in telling them our thoughts, it's best to be gentle whenever we critique someone. We know there are similar idiosyncrasies and flaws in our own lives, and we'd like people to be gentle with us.

Sometimes my friends' actions are really unusual, but I will be very gentle if I feel the need to offer constructive criticism.

A different sense of time

"One must learn a different . . . sense of time, one that depends more on small amounts than big ones."

— SISTER MARY PAUL

How often do we put off starting something new because we're waiting for that magic date "when we have more time"? We're not sure when that day will come. Often, it never does. Most changes happen incrementally. We can start small, not committing a lot of time to a new habit, venture, or activity. We can begin the shift now, using little bits of time that we find throughout our week.

I don't need a lot of time to start something new. I can commit small amounts of time to learn about it and give it a try. Even 10 minutes can be enough if I dedicate those minutes to something specific.

Eliminate needless wants

"*Reduce the complexity of life by eliminating the needless wants of life, and the labors of life reduce themselves.*"

—⌒ EDWIN WAY TEALE

How often do we set ourselves up for stress by over-committing our time and resources? A large purchase requires a loan with terms that demand longer work hours. Too many evening commitments leave us with no time for family or solitude. We are spent—and we did the spending!

We can begin to reverse the process immediately. Say "no" to an extra time drain. Decide against a large purchase. It's a big change in thinking, but the rewards are great. We wake up one day realizing we have more time and presence of mind to enjoy what really matters.

There are ways I can downsize my life to live better and happier within my means.

A measure of one's health

"When you have worn out your shoes, the strength of the shoe leather has passed into the fiber of your body. I measure your health by the number of shoes and hats and clothes you have worn out."

— RALPH WALDO EMERSON

We are on this planet to learn about it, live with it, engage with it. Our bodies are at their best when we're interacting closely with the earth. That only happens if we're willing to get a little messy. Whether we head out the door to climb a mountain or take a walk around a nearby pond, the process of being fully present in our bodies as we enjoy the natural world works wonders for our physical and mental health.

Each step I take as I hike, run, or climb infuses me with joy and health.

All in moderation

"Be moderate in order to taste the joys of life in abundance."

—⌒ EPICURUS

We can make our favorite pleasures even more special by moderating our delight. A small bowl of ice cream, an occasional video game, a special vacation to a distant place, a nice dinner for a friend's birthday, an afternoon off to go fishing. When it's something we don't get to do every day, we are alert to the nuances of the pleasure. We appreciate it more.

The moderate path also allows wider array of experience. Rather than keeping to the same routine every day, we make time for the exceptional and unusual.

I can think of one activity that I've never tried but would like to. I'll make time for that this week. I can also think of another enjoyment that I delight in but have done so often that it's become mundane; I will try leaving it out of my schedule for a while.

275

Hard-won goals

"Life affords no higher pleasure than that of surmounting difficulties."

—⌒ SAMUEL JOHNSON

Whenever we set a goal, whether it is for the day or for the year, unforeseen obstacles can come up. Sometimes it seems easiest to abandon the dream or replace it with something else. There is great satisfaction in tapping the creativity and endurance to keep going and overcome the challenge. A hard-won accomplishment is something to be celebrated.

I have the energy and ability to face the challenges in my life right now. I will take time to ponder a new way to get to my dream. Some of my friends and family might have a few good ideas, too.

Focus

" *There is time enough for everything in the course of the day if you do but one thing at once; but there is not time enough in the year if you will do two things at a time.* **"**

—⌘ LORD CHESTERFIELD

All too often, we find ourselves talking on the phone while walking the dog and thinking not of the person we're speaking to (or the dog!), but of a project waiting at home. Our technologies and lifestyles are dedicated to making ourselves more efficient, but much of the time they simply leave us feeling rushed. And tired.

A rushed and hurried spirit makes it hard to focus. A lack of focus means poor attention and mistakes. In the end, our hyper-efficiency makes us inefficient and dissatisfied. We can break the cycle by tackling one task at a time.

I release all the things I have done and not done today. I choose to complete tasks one at a time with clarity and focus.

Catalysts

"Times of stress and difficulty are seasons of opportunity when the seeds of progress are sown."

— THOMAS F. WOODLOCK

When life goes smoothly, we have no need to change our routine. It's only when we enter a season of challenge that we begin to re-think everything we take for granted. That re-evaluation affects not only the issues directly related to the specific crisis; it tends to overflow into the rest of life as well.

Our attitude opens; we become teachable. In that teachable place, it is easier to change our mind and actions. We are more willing to listen and try another approach. Then, real progress begins.

The difficulties I am experiencing can awaken me to opportunities for change and healthier ways to live.

Tested peace

"*In truth, to attain to interior peace, one must be willing to pass through the contrary to peace.*"

—SWAMI BRAHMANANDA

The people we admire for being unshakeable often are individuals who have gone through hard times and come out shining. Whether it is the loss of a loved one, a severe illness, a failed business, or any other shattering moment, those seasons of grief and starting over tend to cause us to re-evaluate every aspect of life.

That re-evaluation leads to a solid sense of identity. We can quickly identify which factors in life are "small stuff," not worth worrying about. Peace takes root in this process. It is possible, though, to go through a time of re-evaluation without any dramatic catalyst. We can make a choice to embrace the "contrary to peace," knowing the rewards on the other side.

I am thankful for the times that shake my sense of peace; they lead to even deeper and stronger peace.

Love is anti-political

"Love, by its very nature, is unworldly, and it is for this reason rather than its rarity that it is not only apolitical but anti-political, perhaps the most powerful of all anti-political human forces."

—HANNAH ARENDT

Political actions are tied to status, influence, and power. Love, on the other hand, is concerned chiefly about the welfare of others. Love makes decisions that would be unjustifiable from the perspective of political gain.

Sacrificing immediate reward for long-term hopes, love sets aside its own needs. Love knows only the present moment and is shamelessly unconcerned about running out. It is a verb—entirely active. The language of love is movement; it doesn't rely on defined words and knows nothing of policy or regulation.

I welcome joyful acts of love in my relationship. I will listen and watch for creative ways to love the people in my life.

Delight in laughter

"I love myself when I am laughing."
— ZORA NEALE HURSTON

Laughter is both a result of and a cause for loving ourselves. It lightens the atmosphere around us and transforms us internally. It can bring gentleness to a heavy time or increase the delight in a happy moment. In laughter, we find greater contentment and a sense of hope and joy about ourselves, others, and the situation we're in.

I am thankful for the gift of laughter. I am pleased with myself and others when we share a good laugh.

It's the people

> *" The great difference between voyages rests not in ships but in the people you meet on them. "*
>
> —⟡ AMELIA BURR

We might go somewhere exhilarating with friends, only to return months later on a quiet couples' retreat. We go to coffee with a new friend and find ourselves laughing until tears run down our cheeks; when we take a loved one out for lunch, we spend the time reminiscing about a bittersweet memory.

The unique personalities in our lives affects the voyages we take together. One experience is lighthearted and playful, another takes on a more contemplative tone. The people we work with and love collaborate with us to create each unique experience.

I value the range of ideas and emotions that I experience both through developing new friendships and caring for long-standing relationships.

Action requires faith

❝It is faith, and not reason, which impels men to action . . . Intelligence is content to point out the road, but never drives us along it.❞

—✺ DR. ALEXIS CARREL

It is often said that knowing is half the battle, but when we are considering a major risk or lifestyle change, knowing what to do may seem like only ten percent of the battle! We think we know precisely what we need to do or say, but then we procrastinate in the face of what we don't know.

The spark of faith provides the catalyst for movement. At some point, we recognize that acquiring more information will not help us move forward. We move forward only by taking an initial faith-filled step. In the process, that first step also helps build our sense of faith. Like muscle, it grows with use.

I choose to exercise my faith by taking action in an area of my life where I have stalled. I will grow my sense of faith by using it.

Limitless faith

"Faith is a sounder guide than reason. Reason can go only so far, but faith has no limits."

—⌘ BLAISE PASCAL

We use reason to determine the little nuances of how to complete a task or make a hope a reality, but only faith provides the catalyst to take the first step. Faith adds the extra spark that can lead to a journey reason never would have conceived.

I am open to listening to the small voice of faith. I see surprising possibilities and welcome them.

Greatness in small things

> "I long to accomplish a great and noble task, but it is my chief duty to accomplish small tasks as if they were great and noble."
>
> —HELEN KELLER

It's encouraging and humbling to hear such a courageous and inspiring individual make this claim. What if we were to take this as a commission to carry out our daily tasks with renewed purpose? What would happen to the quality of our work? Our days? Our life?

It's only when we take small tasks seriously, with honor and dedication, that we open ourselves to even greater possibilities. As we learn and master small ventures, we ready ourselves for more—and we discover greater meaning along the way.

I am entrusted with both great and small tasks. My respect and care in approaching a task is consistent, no matter what I am doing.

Risk and reward of love

"Age does not protect you from love but love to some extent protects you from age."

—◌ JEANNE MOREAU

Love is risky. We sometimes conclude we know better than to try to increase our capacity to love. The hurts that can be a part of the adventure of love leave us feeling old and weary.

Love has a will and existence of its own. It shows up at any age, knocking on the heart's door at the most surprising moment. Then, when we are wise enough to resist the urge to hide and instead open the door, we discover that love makes us feel young again.

I am grateful for the way that love, in all forms of relationship and connection, keeps me feeling young.

Trusting yourself

"As soon as you trust yourself, you will know how to live."

— JOHANN VON GOETHE

So much of our day-to-day tension and stress comes from our own uncertainties. We're not sure we'll make the right choice or that we will be able to complete the tasks at hand. We worry about making mistakes. As we grow to trust our own capacity and ability to choose wisely, decisions are easier. Life begins to be fun. The moment we quit scrutinizing ourselves so harshly and release ourselves to simply try, the path becomes clear.

I trust my judgment and my abilities. There are big choices ahead, but I have what it takes to make them. I will enjoy the process.

Choosing our thoughts

> "*If we are not responsible for the thoughts that pass our doors, we are at least responsible for those we admit and entertain.*"
>
> —◌ CHARLES B. NEWCOMB

We think all sorts of random thoughts during the course of a day, some inspired by movies we've seen or books we've read. Even the food we eat might affect some of our attitudes and thoughts. But, not everything that pops into the mind's eye is a true expression of our character.

Thoughts are the first step toward action. Some ideas are great little brainstorms; cultivating those thoughts might lead to trying something new that will be good for us. Other thoughts are best left alone. We can choose to ignore random thoughts that are unproductive or harmful to ourselves or others.

I will be more diligent and intentional about which thoughts I admit and entertain in my mind. I can choose which ones become my meditation and then my source of action.

Dignity and discipline

"*Self-respect is the fruit of discipline; the sense of dignity grows with the ability to say 'no' to oneself.*"

— ABRAHAM JOSHUA HESCHEL

As we begin on a spiritual path, we may start out wrestling with ourselves. Conflicting desires and hopes leave us feeling confused and frustrated. Decision-making feels like a roller coaster when we're not entirely sure what we want or who we are.

As we mature and get more comfortable in our own skin, we realize how freeing it is to be able to say "no" to random thoughts or impulses. It doesn't have to be a drama. Just a simple, "no, that's not for me," will suffice. Capable of calmly saying "no" to a distraction without letting ourselves be disappointed, we continue on our way in peace.

I am glad I can say "no" to myself. I can wisely choose and direct my own actions.

Deep wisdom

"There is deep wisdom within our very flesh, if we can only come to our senses and feel it."

— ELIZABETH A. BEHNKE

We call it intuition or gut feeling. Our ancestors instinctively knew how to navigate their world and meet their daily needs. When we juggle modern work and schedules, our lives tend to be oriented more to the world between our ears. We make daily choices based on deadlines, not hunches.

It takes a strong act of will to regularly check in with what our bodies are telling us. With all the decisions that come at us each day and all the creative problem-solving required of us, practicing intuition may be more important than ever.

I have more than enough information for most of my decisions. When reasoning alone comes up short, I will try listening to my body and make a choice based on intuition.

Tomorrow's dreams
start today

"*Begin to be today what you want to
be tomorrow.*"

—⊱ SAINT JEROME

It takes time for a habit to become ingrained or
for us to master a skill. Looking back, we can
see how attitudes we embraced and options we
chose a year ago, five years ago, or a dozen years
ago are still affecting us today. When we want to
change our lives, we must begin the legacy for
ourselves today.

Whether we want to work on strengthening
a character trait or growing a talent, there are
small actions we can take right now. Those seeds
of action will take root, grow, and eventually
mature into a great forest of life. That will happen only if we are bold enough to start small.

I have a dream for myself that I've been putting
off. This week, I will find one way to take a small
step toward that dream.

Strength of momentum

"The first step binds one to the second."

— FRENCH PROVERB

Momentum is an amazing force. Once we begin a project, it creates its own energy and we keep at it. Once we take a risk and introduce ourselves to a new person, the conversation tumbles out and evolves into a new friendship. When we face a challenge and try a few ways to overcome it, the solution suddenly becomes clear.

The hardest part is simply beginning, choosing a direction and then taking the first step. After that, it is easier to discern the next move. It's even easier to adjust our course—once we are in motion.

The first step is always the most daunting. I know I'll feel more confident, and the next step will be much clearer, once I begin.

Choose happiness

"Happiness is a conscious choice, not an automatic response."

—◌ MILDRED BARTHEL

We would rather view happiness as something that comes to us from the outside. It often looks like that when an event occurs that makes us happy. But, we choose what we delight in. We also choose whether or not we see the reasons for delight all around us. When we recognize happiness as a conscious choice, we can begin to turn happiness into a habit and, eventually, an ingrained attitude.

I choose happiness right now.

True sophistication

"*Simplicity is the ultimate sophistication.***"**
—◌ LEONARDO DA VINCI

Systems, schedules, projects, deadlines, traffic, broken equipment . . . our lives can feel cluttered and stressful at times. Our sophisticated technologies were meant to make life easier, but they often complicate things. Similarly, we may create stress in our relationships, making them more complicated than they actually are.

Caught up in how something *should* work, we miss out on how it *could* work. In our work and relationships, it is good to take a step back from any challenge and see if there is a simple but overlooked answer.

I wonder if I am complicating things in my life. I will look for the simple solution.

Who do you want to be?

"First say to yourself what you would be, and then do what you have to do."

— EPICTETUS

We get caught up in the tumble of life events. Sometimes we find ourselves running on autopilot for days—maybe even years! We must not thoughtlessly wear yet another hat—it's likely to send us into the same autopilot mode; only the clothing will have changed.

It's vital that we take time for reflection first, look in the mirror and ask, "Who do I really want to be?" With that picture of ourselves, we can decide what to do next to begin our journey toward our new self.

Who do I want to be in five years? In ten years? I can see that other self, and it may be very different from who I am today. I will answer that question and then begin to walk toward the new me.

Few wants

“*Wealth consists not in having great possessions but in having few wants.*”

—§ ESTHER DE WAAL

Wealth is relative. Cultures vary in their currencies and status symbols. What looks like not much to one might be a sign of great wealth to another. The one universal, however, is that those who chase wealth seem to have a constant desire to have more.

It is not bad to have possessions and financial abundance. But, if we are commanded by our desire for more, we will never be satisfied. Those who genuinely feel wealthy often root themselves in gratitude and constantly trim their list of wants. Essentially, they are satisfied with simple things and are gratefully delighted by any extras that come their way.

I can see how much wealth I have. I choose to be grateful for these good things and will be thoughtful before adding to my list of wants.

Gleanings each day

"True wisdom lies in gathering the precious things out of each day as it goes by."

—⟶ E.S. BOUTON

Life is a classroom. We learn whether we intend to or not, but it's more fun and far more engaging when we choose to fully participate as students. Each day, we can watch for the little gems and lessons that life gives us. We can ask questions about things that don't seem to make sense. We can research, like archeologists or explorers. Most of all, we can be thankful for all our teachers—other people, circumstances, animals, and nature. There are precious gifts everywhere; we just need to watch for them, reach out, and accept.

I received several precious gifts and life lessons today. I will take some time to recount them and be thankful.

Using small amounts of time

"An earnest purpose finds time, or makes it. It seizes on spare moments, and turns fragments to golden account."

—∽ WILLIAM ELLERY CHANNING

We might be finishing a project, learning a musical instrument, or planning a big family event. When we're excited about something, we know how to use our spare time. We tap that sense of inner motivation and discover there are free moments throughout the day we can use to make a phone call, jot a note, or practice a few bars of a song. The big goal can be broken down into small pieces that fit into those little pockets of time.

It's interesting how efficient I become when I'm motivated by a deadline or something I really enjoy. I will look for, and make use of, free moments throughout my day.

Those who tell you the truth

"There are only two people who can tell you the truth about yourself—an enemy who has lost his temper and a friend who loves you dearly."

—ℰ ANTISTHENES

We would rather hear the truth from someone who loves us, although it can be awkward to hear it from anyone. An enemy will state it without mincing words, and may hope to use the truth to hurt us. Friends will pad the truth with love and a desire to see us grow.

No matter who speaks the truth to us, we can be self-controlled as we listen to their words. We can hear them out without becoming defensive and acknowledge that we'll give their thoughts consideration. We can set boundaries about which issues we're willing to deal with right now and which ones will need to wait.

I don't always like to hear the truth, especially if the person saying it is lording it over me. I do want to grow, however, so I will listen to truth, regardless of who speaks it.

Endless forgiveness

> "*Love is an act of endless forgiveness, a tender look which becomes a habit.*"
>
> — PETER USTINOV

As dear as they are to us, our loved ones have habits and flaws that can get under our skin. We forgive them daily for these little irritations. We realize they accept and forgive our idiosyncrasies, too. Over time, a well-worn gentle acceptance covers the edges of irritation. We forgive like breathing, and do so with genuine warmth.

I forgive the irritations caused by my family and friends. Love is strong enough to overlook all our little faults.

A responsibility to care

"Provision for others is a fundamental responsibility of human life."

— WOODROW WILSON

Our most admirable moments are in times of trial, when one person sacrifices their time, resources, or safety to put another person first.

We don't have to wait for a major crisis to cultivate that attitude. Every day there are people on the planet struggling. It's a privilege to reach out with whatever we have. As we help, we remember we are not islands; we all need each other.

It is my responsibility to look out for the needs of others. As we individually recognize this, we collectively begin to help heal the pain and need around us.

The goal of mentorship

"First, teach a person to develop to the point of his limitations and then—pfft!—break the limitations."

—◇ VIOLA SPOLIN

The most powerful thing we can teach another person is the way to break through their own limits. Whether we are mentoring a child or a contemporary, everyone benefits from that moment of realization. "Wow, I didn't know I could do that!" they exclaim. It's an amazing feeling; they know now that the sky—and nothing below it—is the limit. It's a great feeling for us, too; we just brought a little more freedom into the world.

There is nothing more satisfying than helping someone meet and exceed their goals.

Fate and free will

> *"Life is like a game of cards. The hand that is dealt you represents determinism; the way you play it is free will."*
>
> —⟳ JAWAHARLAL NEHRU

Are our lives determined by fate? Or, do we master our own destinies? If we take an honest look at our path to this point, it seems like a colorful mix of both. This thought will unnerve any philosophical purist, but how else can we explain our experience?

There are moments that appear to be orchestrated by powers outside us. We've been baffled by challenges and mercies alike that have transformed us and made us who we are today. Then, there are just as many moments when the choice was in our hands, and our act of will made a real difference.

I don't understand providence and synchronicity. I know there are events and forces out of my control. But, I will be diligent about the "cards" that are in my hand. I'll play as wisely as I can.

Sufficient conclusion

"Life is the art of drawing sufficient conclusions from insufficient premises."

—— SAMUEL BUTLER

"How can I decide? I need more facts. It's too much of a risk," we say. If we don't make a decision, the opportunity may pass us by.

Each day, we make judgment calls without having every possible fact. We keep moving forward, even though few premises are certain. For the most part, we simply ignore the uncertainty, but, occasionally, when we're making a big decision, it gets to us. We want to be completely sure, but it's not possible. We examine all the data, then make our best guess.

My decisions do not have to be perfect in order to be sound. It's not always possible to research every possible outcome. I will consider all the factors I'm aware of and then make the best decision I can.

Loss of empathy

❝*We are cold to others only when we are dull in ourselves.*❞

— WILLIAM HAZLITT

Our sensitivity to the needs of others can be an accurate barometer for the health of our souls. If we no longer feel a tug of compassion and concern when hearing about another's hurts, we know we've grown a bit callused. What's going on in our spiritual life that may be causing this? Perhaps we are over-working, wrestling with our own hurts, or not taking enough time for the things that delight our spirit. There is some part of us that needs nourishment and healing. Until we give our bodies what they need, we have too many walls up; it will be hard for us to empathize.

If I find myself reacting coldly to someone else's problems, I will take a moment to measure my own spiritual pulse. It may be that I haven't been taking care of myself very well.

Priceless heart

❝ *To wear your heart on your sleeve isn't a very good plan; you should wear it inside, where it functions best.* ❞

—◌ MARGARET THATCHER

Our deepest thoughts and most vulnerable feelings are priceless; we must treasure them. Like a locked diary or a private study, we only share them with certain people who have earned our trust; they will handle our heart with care. In our public lives, it's natural and appropriate that we are a little more guarded and selective about what we disclose.

Honesty is one thing, but telling all to everyone is excessive. I will carefully choose to whom I entrust my heart.

Spontaneity

> *Spontaneity is the quality of being able to do something just because you feel like it at the moment, of trusting your instincts, of taking yourself by surprise and snatching from the clutches of your well-organized routine a bit of unscheduled pleasure.*
>
> —◇ RICHARD IANNELLI

We call a friend we haven't spoken with for years and ask to go for coffee. We pass by the same store on our way home every day, but this time, we decide to go in and have a look. It's cleaning day at home, but the day is sunny and we decide to take a walk around the neighborhood instead. These are the moments that add color, richness, and meaning to our lives. Rather than stifling spontaneity, it's good to listen to its playful call and gladly follow.

I can be spontaneous once in a while. I come away with a smile on my face, and I remember how important it is to let myself play.

Likeness and difference

" *There is space within sisterhood for likeness and difference, for the subtle differences that challenge and delight; there is space for disappointment— and surprise.* "

— CHRISTINE DOWNING

We grow irritated at our loved ones' differences. Why can't they see things the way we do? But, their differences are what bring life and surprise into our relationship. When we loosen the reins of control and let each other be individuals, we grow together and appreciate the similarities and contrasts, the joys and challenges.

My loved ones and I have a lot in common. We're different, too. I will give them room to be who they are.

Peace through education

"Establishing lasting peace is the work of education; all politics can do is keep us out of war."

—⌁ MARIA MONTESSORI

Too often, political efforts can barely do just that—keep us out of war. Follow the cause-and-effect chain leading up to war and we find a root cause tangled up in a lack of education—a total breakdown in understanding, a lack of knowledge about the rest of the world. If powerful nations are to make peace with other nations, perhaps the first act is to take an interest in equipping teachers, founding schools, and letting our students learn about each other.

I can do my part to learn more about other cultures and countries, and help others learn as well. I'm just one person, but if many of us take time to educate ourselves, we can make a difference.

An ounce of help

> "*When a person is down in the world, an ounce of help is better than a pound of preaching.*"
> —⟡ EDWARD BULWER-LYTTON

"Wow, how did they get themselves into that mess?" we wonder about someone who's having emotional, financial, or relationship troubles. If we chat with them, it's tempting to point out what we view as the cause of all their trouble.

Perhaps it makes us feel a little more secure. We would never make such a choice, right? Yet, we've had some low days, too. We remember that others' lectures were not helpful at all; they only made us feel worse. What prompted us to start recovering was a listening and accepting presence, a hug, encouraging words, a quiet helping hand.

When someone I know gets into a low spot, I won't persist in looking for the cause of it all. I will be the listening ear and voice of encouragement.

Teaching kids selflessness

"*Giving kids clothes and food is one thing, but it's much more important to teach them that other people besides themselves are important and that the best thing they can do with their lives is to use them in the service of other people.*"

—DOLORES HUERTA

As we mentor young people, it's easy to focus mainly on their more immediate and tangible needs. We encourage them in their studies and personal activities, take them shopping, and introduce them to new aspects of popular culture.

But children need to be taught how to see outside their own needs and interests, to notice the needs of others. Teaching this is a vital task. We need to do it on many levels—through words, our own actions, and giving opportunities to practice.

If I'm concerned that a child I know seems a bit self-centered, I won't fault the child. Perhaps there is a creative way I can model and teach service to them.

Forgiving a friend

"It is easier to forgive an enemy than a friend."
— MADAME DOROTHEE DELUZY

We expect a foe to hurt or offend us. They have a history of doing that, and we would be surprised if they didn't! We forgive them simply to keep our own sanity; we don't want to be dragged down by bitterness. If a trusted friend or loved one hurts us, it is much harder to forgive. We keep returning to the disappointment and the breach of trust. We expected them to be kind and understanding, to think of our needs—and they didn't. It is important that we forgive our dear ones, so we can begin the work of rebuilding trust.

It's not easy to forgive when I've been hurt by someone I love, but the relationship is important to me. I will practice forgiveness and be open to restoring trust.

Maximum efficiency

" *Don't be fooled by the calendar. There are only as many days in the year as you make use of. One man gets only a week's value out of a year while another man gets a full year's value out of a week.* "

— CHARLES RICHARDS

They say that if we want something done fast, we should give it to a busy person. Busy people need to use their time efficiently—they don't have enough of it to sweat the small stuff! Some people seem to get a year of work done in a week. Of course, they can end up so busy that overwork and lack of rest lead to inefficiencies. There is a happy medium. People who have a handle on both efficiency and healthy personal boundaries are the ones who make purposeful use of all their days.

There are areas in my life where I'm wasting time "sweating the small stuff" through worry, perfectionism, and unimportant activities. I can cut back on all of that.

Fresh air, fresh perspective

"A vigorous five-mile walk will do more good for an unhappy but otherwise healthy adult than all the medicine and psychology in the world."

— PAUL DUDLEY WHITE

There is a time for wise counsel and basic medical care, but, sometimes, a good brisk walk is all it takes to bring our mood back into balance. We may have a poor attitude or we may be discouraged because we're standing a little too close to a problem. Movement and a change of scenery can be a rewarding way to get both fresh oxygen and fresh thinking into our mind.

If I'm spinning my wheels on an issue, it may be time to disengage for a little while. I will take a quick walk to renew my perspective.

Listen to the story

"One of the most valuable things we can do to heal one another is listen to each other's stories."

— REBECCA FALLS

We love to look for ways to fix a sad story. Even when someone shares a happy story, we may take over the conversation by comparing the experience to our own. It can be quite an act of will to force ourselves to simply listen, but that is what helps heal. It's also a great compliment we can pay another person.

Listening quietly, asking the occasional question, we relinquish the spotlight for a moment and let the storyteller shine. In the telling of their story, they often find their own answers and discover a new level of care and acceptance.

I don't need to fix the problem or provide my own opinion when people share their stories with me. I can simply listen, showing them I care and am fully present.

Enjoy life

> *"All animals except man know that the principle business of life is to enjoy it."*
>
> —☙ SAMUEL BUTLER

Animals live purely in the moment. We've all seen how a dog greets his master with unabashed joy, or marveled at wild animals playing, seemingly for the sheer fun of it. Other creatures know intimately the stress of immediate survival, but we humans appear to be the only ones capable of worry. We create our own internal stress over things we can't control and that may not even come to pass. How much happiness do we forfeit in the face of imagined threats?

It is a release to remember to breathe, look around ourselves, and recognize all the good in our lives. While having real struggle, fear, or sadness, it is wise to find the joy in the middle of it.

I see and experience all the beauty and pleasure in my life right now. I will do one activity tomorrow just for the fun of it.

Expressing all

"It is only by expressing all that is inside that purer and purer streams come."

—◯ BRENDA UELAND

It might feel safer to keep some of our thoughts inside. Yet, as with any creative process, our spiritual growth often requires us to face, acknowledge, and find safe ways to express all that is inside. Anger, fear, and regret are emotions that seem too dark to share with anyone. "I'm fine," we say to ourselves and others.

Kept inside, those feelings can block the flow of growth and change. There are useful ways to work through our darker feelings. We can journal, or talk with a safe friend or counselor. There may be a physical exercise that expresses it better than words. Once the internal feelings are released, fresh, renewed thinking can flow.

I acknowledge the places in my soul that seem blocked. I will look at these areas and listen for any feelings I need to express.

Body, mind, and spirit

"Health is a large word. It embraces not the body only, but the mind and spirit as well . . . and not today's pain or pleasure alone, but the whole being and outlook of a man."

—◊ JAMES H. WEST

Work life. Home life. Exercise. Friends. Spiritual community. We look at life as if it were a compartmentalized day planner.

But we were not meant to be fragmented people. A spiritual challenge will affect our physical health; heavy decisions will test our spiritual beliefs; physical exercise will increase our creativity. Similarly, our relationships affect each other. Health involves bringing all these elements into harmony.

All the aspects of my life are like colorful spokes of one wheel. As I think about my health, I'll look for overlooked connections and make changes to bring more balance into my life.

Open to epiphany

"Not knowing when the dawn will come, I open every door."

— EMILY DICKINSON

Creative inspiration—whether in work, play, or relationships—is not something that can be predicted. We can set the stage for it, however. We can create lives that are welcoming to inspiration. We can give ourselves time to let our minds wander and play. We can open every door within and—although not every door holds the epiphany we seek—we will see the fresh idea arrive through one of them.

I enjoy taking time for creative thought. I will look for and consider new possibilities, even if they seem a little odd. It may lead to the new dawn I seek.

Accepting yourself

"To accept ourselves as we are means to value our imperfections as much as our perfections."

—SANDRA BIERIG

It's easy to celebrate our strengths. Yet, in many ways, we only see our strengths in light of our weaknesses. We usually discover our imperfections as we interact in community and see others' strengths. Our flaws are precious. By taking care of ourselves, and through the kindness of our loved ones, we protect our imperfections and see them as part of our vulnerability and humanity. We find ways to care for others in the areas where they are imperfect.

I value both my flaws and my strengths. My weaknesses are precious quirks. I can learn to laugh about them and care for them gently.

Inner worth

"No one can figure out your worth but you."

— PEARL BAILEY

Others can encourage and compliment us, but only we have the power to fully recognize our own value. No amount of praise will change the opinion of someone who believes he or she has little worth.

When we are thoroughly convinced of our own worth, we are unstoppable. Undue criticism and difficult times may rattle us, but nothing can shatter that inner knowledge.

I am precious. I am of infinite value just the way I am.

Sailing through circumstances

> "It is our relationship to circumstances that determines their influence over us. The same wind that carries one vessel into port may blow another off shore."
>
> —⌐ CHRISTIAN BOVEE

People experienced in sailing know that reading the wind and water is an art. We can plot a course, but the weather is not always predictable. A wise captain will find a way to work with the changing factors, harnessing them to get the boat where it needs to go. Good sailors know when to wait out a storm, or when to set anchor and wait for a better breeze. Like sailing, life is a constant interaction with shifting variables. Will we harness them to our advantage, or let them toss us about? It's our choice.

I am not afraid of the wind blowing at my boat. I can use it to fill my sails and take me where I want to go.

Gifts of love and time

❝*Love and time—those are the only two things in all the world and all of life that cannot be bought, but only spent.*❞

—◦ GARY JENNINGS

Love and time are essential components of who we are. It is always a risk to share our love and time; we are literally sharing ourselves. We cannot recover that gift—we're not meant to. So, we are thoughtful and wise about when and with whom we share love and time. We cannot expect these gifts to be returned according to our personal desires.

It is always worthwhile to take the risk. Love and time may never come back to us in identical form, but eventually we will be rewarded in surprising ways.

Sometimes it feels risky to share my love and time, but I will decide thoughtfully about when to do so and hold loosely my hope for reciprocation.

Cultivate happiness

"Happiness must be cultivated. It is like character. It is not a thing to be safely let alone for a moment, or it will run to weeds."

— ELIZABETH STUART PHELPS

We tend to think of happiness as something we come upon through pleasing circumstances, but the happiest people regard it as a character trait. It is an attitude, a view of life they build brick-by-brick through daily choices. Every situation can have a negative spin. In each moment, we can look for the ray of light, too.

The source of happiness is not from without; it's from within. It means choosing to look for joy in every moment.

I can choose to be happy. I will begin practicing right now. I can be glad about something I am thankful for in my life—or for no particular reason at all.

Ingredients for happiness

"Caring about others, running the risk of feeling, and leaving an impact on people, bring happiness."

——⌀ RABBI HAROLD KUSHNER

We all have memories of happy moments. Those moments may have involved some aspect of vulnerability, too—the time we shared deep conversation with a loved one and they received it well, the day we started a project that was too big for us and dear friends arrived to help out, or all the outdoor adventures with childhood pals. Those were happy times.

The recipe for happiness is fairly simple: relationship, honesty, and a dash of healthy risk. When things turn stagnant, we should find one small way to bring those ingredients back into our life.

My own happiness is directly tied to my willingness to take risks in relationships, to reach out and interact with others and the world around me.

Walking toward inspiration

"If you are seeking creative ideas, go out walking. Angels whisper to a man when he goes for a walk."

—⌒ RAYMOND INMON

There's nothing better than physical activity to spark creative thought. A research scientist once commented to a writer friend, "Whenever I sit down to write a summary, I get distracted. It seems like I need at least an hour of cleaning my house before I can actually write. What can I do to focus better?"

The writer replied, "Wash a few more dishes! The cleaning is probably how you get your creativity sparked. I always plan for some movement or exercise before working. That's how my mind gets ideas."

The next time I'm stuck on a decision, creative task, or conflict, I'll remember to get out for a little fresh air. Maybe some fresh ideas will come to me, too.

Simple cures

"A good laugh and a long sleep are the best cures in the doctor's book."

— IRISH PROVERB

Modern science now proves it: A poor attitude and poor sleep both can be hard on our immune systems. Conversely, laughter produces endorphins that are good for our bodies and sleep gives the body time to repair and renew itself.

Laughter has always been great medicine. We've known this for ages. Whenever we feel we're fighting something, we can let our bodies sleep it off. Sometimes the best cures are the ones based in simple folk wisdom.

When I feel I might be getting sick, I'll remember some simple self-care. Perhaps my life has gotten a little too busy and my body is reminding me to slow down and enjoy.

Gut feeling

> **A trembling in the bones may carry a more convincing testimony than the dry documented deductions of the brain.**
>
> —⟡ LLEWELYN POWERS

We trust most often in logic, but it's good to listen to the body, too. With the voice of sheer instinct, the body gives us honest messages. Too easily, we try to reason our way around a healthy gut feeling, but the body does not play games with us.

Body and mind often confirm each other. "I don't have a good feeling about this place," we think. Meanwhile, we've unconsciously stepped back toward the door. We're doing the math in our mind while our body has already made and executed a choice.

I have a healthy instinct and am grateful for the gut feelings that have helped get me through some difficult situations. I will listen to and heed the signs my body gives me.

Small things, great love

"*To show great love for God and our neighbor, we need not do great things. It is how much love we put in the doing that makes our offering something beautiful for God.*"

—⊙ MOTHER TERESA

We can get hung up on wanting to solve the world's problems. We want to do something grandiose that affects thousands. Greatness starts much smaller, though; it begins with our capacity to love.

Do we have a heart for children's literacy? We can read to the little boy next door. Concerned about global poverty? A local job skills center may need volunteers. Overwhelmed by the refugee crisis? Our willingness to give a small donation or a listening ear is all it takes to spark change.

When I give of myself with genuine love, I contribute to the kindness and compassion in the world. God is present in the love that is given; that is all that matters.

Stillness first

"One's action ought to come out of an achieved stillness: not to be a mere rushing on."

—D.H. LAWRENCE

Much of our busy-ness is just busy work. Once in a while, when we go on vacation or if we take a couple of sick days, we discover that the multitude of day-to-day tasks we hurry to complete can be set aside.

In the stillness, we find a creativity that often is sacrificed to the normal schedule. That creativity is aware of which decisions and actions really matter. To rest and consider—this is important to being human. Hurry begets more artificial rush and stress. Stillness naturally yields wise action and contentment.

I have time to be still, to create a peaceful moment where I can think and ponder before deciding what I will do with my day.

Focus on the remedy

"*Don't find fault. Find a remedy.*"

—⟶ HENRY FORD

Faults can be glaring, as if a giant spotlight is shining on them. We make progress when we deliberately open our focus to include all the resources available to remedy our faults. Brainstorming, we consider any possibility in the hope of finding one that is feasible.

Then, we give ourselves permission to experiment. It will take trial and error. We will learn from mistakes. But, even while making mistakes, we have broken free of the narrow focus on the fault alone.

When I see a problem in part of my life, I will be quick to look for ways to remedy it, rather than focus solely on the problem.

Body language

"Movement never lies. It is a barometer telling the state of the soul's weather."

— MARTHA GRAHAM

Body language is loud. Just watch someone who is uncomfortable with a conversation. They lean away ever so slightly, and cross their arms. We recognize the language in many postures. We grow concerned about a friend who is walking with her face looking down. When someone leans in to listen closer to us, we know they're taking us seriously.

A furrowed brow. A quickened stride. An outstretched arm pointing to the seat nearby. Hands massaging the forehead, rubbing the eyes. A hug. We are all fluent in body language, and we know it speaks louder than words.

Today, I'll pay closer attention to the messages people give through their movement. I'll pay closer attention to my own, too.

Forgive and be forgiven

"He that cannot forgive others breaks the bridge over which he must pass himself; for every man has need to be forgiven."

—🗢 THOMAS FULLER

Every culture has some variant of the Golden Rule: Treat others the way you'd like to be treated. All of humanity's laws could be summed up in that, yet we come up short living this practice on a daily basis. It would be wise to add one more guiding principle to it: Forgive others as you wish to be forgiven. If we make a commitment to both rules, much heartache can be avoided in our relationships.

I will forgive others, not only to release myself from the weight of feeling offended, but also because I hope others will forgive me. I know I will need forgiveness myself at some point.

We receive when we give

"*A bit of fragrance always clings to the hand that gives roses.*"

—⁊ CHINESE PROVERB

When we take the risk of giving of ourselves, we receive something in return. A river channels water to other lands, but the banks along the way benefit, too. The lessons we learn, the joy of the other person, the satisfaction of realizing we've done something truly meaningful—these are priceless gifts that come back to us. Like a sweet fragrance, those gifts emanate from us. Others notice something seems different. We are shining.

It is a delight to give a gift or do something kind. I will take pleasure in the rewards I experience when I share of myself.

Spirit of adventure

"A good traveler has no fixed plans, and is not intent on arriving."

— LAO TZU

Travel itineraries can look as stressful as any work day. To truly enjoy our travels, we need to have the spirit of a wanderer. A guided tour is great to learn facts. But, breaking off the usual path, we may find ourselves on an adventure.

With no specific plan, we head around a bend in the road and find a lane that wasn't on the tourist map. Down that lane is a café. In that café, we strike up a conversation with a local who shares some of the town's history based on his great-grandparents' stories. Here is where the journey begins.

Whether I am on a vacation, or simply traveling through my day-to-day life, I will remember to have a spirit of adventure.

Happiness within

" *The essence of philosophy is that a man should so live that his happiness shall depend as little as possible on external things.* "

—ᏉᏜ EPICTETUS

When happiness depends on circumstances, it is fleeting. There is nothing wrong with enjoying a pleasurable event or interaction, but our joy must not depend on those external factors. We can choose a life philosophy in which our happiness comes from within and is enhanced by the good things all around us.

My happiness comes from within me. Whenever something difficult happens, I can draw from my reserves of happiness. When good things come my way, it only increases the joy I already have.

Fair play

> *Fair play with others is primarily not blaming them for anything that is wrong with us.*
>
> — ERIC HOFFER

When we play fair as adults, it's a lot like the games we played as children. We still need to honor boundaries and rules. Relationships go more smoothly when we are the first to admit our mistakes. We can avoid many relationship impasses by being the first to admit responsibility, rather than being the first to point out a flaw in someone else.

I can play fair. I am secure enough in my relationships to admit when I have gone out of bounds. I don't need to point out the weaknesses in the other person to make myself feel better.

Dependence and self-reliance

> **"** *To character and success, two things,*
> *contradictory as they may seem, must go*
> *together—humble dependence on God and manly*
> *reliance on self.* **"**
>
> —◌ WILLIAM WORDSWORTH

Focus only on getting help, and we begin to lose
our sense of resolve and self-control. Focus only
on self-reliance, and we become arrogant and
merciless. It is not an either/or choice. We need
to be both dependent and self-reliant.

It's a little like walking. In quick turns,
we use both left and right in equal measure.
Similarly, we can be aware of the steady flow of
both our vulnerability and our inner strength.
With both, we stride toward success while
strengthening our character.

I am equally aware of my need for divine guidance
and my own strong resolve.

Healthy physical work

"Why be given a body if you have to keep it shut up in a case like a rare, rare fiddle?"

—◇ KATHERINE MANSFIELD

"My muscles ache," we say the day after a hard workout. "But it's a good kind of sore." We all know the feeling of satisfaction after achieving an exercise goal, hiking far through the woods, or getting some heavy lifting done around the house.

Our bodies were not designed to sit still. After hard work, we feel energized, as if every cell benefited from the extra effort. Indeed, that likely is the case, as the increased circulation cleanses and brings nourishment throughout our body, and the endorphin kick lightens our mood.

Feeling perfectly comfortable all the time isn't necessarily the best. It's good for me to do some healthy physical work, too.

Pick one

> "*If you walk, just walk. If you sit, just sit. But whatever you do, don't wobble.*"
>
> — ANONYMOUS

When the mind or heart is divided about something, it shows. It's no fun to feel unsure, and it's confusing for those around us, too. We need to take time to decide where our allegiances and preferences lie, and then make a commitment to them. Whatever we do then, we do with a sense of security and certainty.

I can make solid, unwavering decisions. I'll take the time to discern what I really want to do and then commit without regret.

Working with limitations

> "*Do what you can, with what you have, where you are.*"
>
> —⌁ THEODORE ROOSEVELT

Wherever we go, whatever we want to do, there will always be limitations. Whether we lack finances, time, or access to opportunity, we can choose to become discouraged by the limitations, or we can brainstorm a way through them.

Perhaps there is no one in our town who can teach us a hobby we would like to learn. We can start by reading a book about it. Perhaps we wish we had a better job, and the search is going poorly. We can grow our skill base in the meantime. Perhaps we don't have the time to drive to the gym right now. We can set aside a half-hour workout each day at home.

I will have a hopeful attitude toward limitations in my life. I can find a creative way to work with them.

A wholehearted attitude

"If you aren't going all the way, why go at all?"
— JOE NAMATH

It's important to put our whole heart into what we're doing. When we're halfhearted, we drag our own energy level down. Feeling uncertain or wavering about our interest and commitment level, we complete the job poorly. It would be better to say "no" and do something else with real commitment. For the sake of those working with us, and for our own sense of pride, we can give each task our all and finish strong. As soon as we make this decision, the choice creates its own enthusiasm and energy.

I have the energy to bring wholehearted enthusiasm to my day-to-day work and my larger personal goals. I will finish strong.

Today is the most important

"Nothing is worth more than this day."
— JOHANN VON GOETHE

Today is the only day we can influence. Right now, we can choose a positive attitude, be grateful, look for joy, smile, or encourage someone. We cannot change the past or control our future, but these present decisions are the building blocks for each day. What did we build today? What will we build tomorrow?

Today is what matters. The moment I'm in right now is the only one I can influence and affect in ways that are in line with my values.

Meaningful work

❝We work not only to produce, but to give value to time.❞

—❧ EUGENE DELACROIX

Most people spend more of their waking hours at their workplace than anywhere else. It's no wonder we are happiest when we have meaningful work. It flows from our strengths and talents; each day we feel we have added some good to the world. We have spent our time in a way that feels valuable to us. Compensation for our contributions completes the circle.

It is frustrating when our job is unpleasant. It can be exhausting to go to work each day when our purpose is only to pay our bills. We can take steps to look for different work, increase our skills so we qualify for a career change, or transform our current work into the right job.

I am thankful for my work and especially grateful if it is work that I am passionate about. If it isn't, I will think of ways to change it or grow it into something better.

Confident navigation

> "*The winds and the waves are always on the side of the ablest navigators.*"
>
> —ᴏ EDWARD GIBBON

Challenges and obstacles in our lives are often out of our control. When we feel overwhelmed and buffeted, we can choose what perspective to take. Are we tossed about at the whim of the weather, or are we actively responding to each change and shift?

If we think of ourselves as navigators, we discover ourselves in the midst of a fantastic adventure. Drawing on our skills and experience, and remembering we are part of a larger team that can help with our tasks, we realize we'll not only get through the wind and waves, we will use them to our advantage.

I can confidently navigate the changes that come my way. I am grateful for the energy and power of the wind and the waves.

Conflict between friends

> *A quarrel between friends, when made up, adds a new tie to friendship, as . . . the callosity formed 'round a broken bone makes it stronger than before.*

— SAINT FRANCIS DE SALES

When a friendship is solid, we're able to speak honestly and even argue with each other. As long as we both honor each other, conflict can actually make our relationship stronger. In fact, an ongoing close relationship with no conflicts may be a little stunted in its growth and maturity.

Recognizing that we are separate people who will not agree on everything gives us the freedom to develop and change while still respecting and accepting each other.

I do not need to be afraid of conflict in my friendships. I can navigate occasional conflicts with loved ones in a way that communicates my respect for them regardless of the outcome.

God's answers

> "*Be thankful that God's answers are wiser than your answers.*"
>
> —☙ WILLIAM CULBERTSON

What a mess we'd be in if we had to know all the right answers! We can paralyze ourselves trying to figure things out. Often, our best solution is trumped by a surprise that winds up being helpful in the long run. There are unseen forces acting upon our lives, and wisdom is often measured out to us as we become ready for it.

It's okay to go forward in life with the little bit of wisdom we have, trusting that more will be revealed as we need it.

I don't have all the answers, and that's okay. I am glad I get to learn and enjoy the answers as I discover them.

Long days

"The longest day is soon ended."

— PLINY THE YOUNGER

Oh, what a long day. Sometimes we hit the end of a day truly exhausted. Perhaps it was physically demanding or drawn out by stress and troubles. Thankfully, all hard days do come to an end. We can retreat to sleep, letting its peace renew us—both body and mind. The day is done. There is no more we can do, and that is a mercy.

The next time I have a long day, I will remember that even the most difficult day ends at some point. I can always look forward to tomorrow as a fresh start.

When we lack experience

> "*I probably hold the distinction of being one movie star who, by all laws of logic, should never have made it. At each stage of my career, I lacked the experience.*"

—⌐ AUDREY HEPBURN

Where experience is lacking, some healthy audacity may do the trick. Perhaps we don't have the exact experience that is needed for a certain task, but we have done a handful of similar things. We're ready for a new challenge, too. Why not give it a try? When we are open to possibility, others pick up on it. Because we believe in ourselves, they feel more confident that we will succeed, too.

I will go into new situations with confidence, curiosity, and the belief that I can do it. Even if I do not get what I want, I will have fun trying.

A sense of beauty

> "A man should hear a little music, read a little poetry, and see a fine picture every day of his life, in order that worldly cares may not obliterate the sense of the beautiful which God has implanted in the human soul."
>
> —JOHANN VON GOETHE

Life is not only the activities of our daily grind. When we take time for beauty and artful expression, we remember that we are not machines. Creativity and beauty remind us that we are ourselves creations, designed for joy. Work can be a means to expand our capacity for wonder, not an end in itself.

I will take some time this week to enjoy art, literature, and craftsmanship. It would be a great way to slow down and appreciate my own creativity.

Creating the self

> **"***The self is not something that one finds. It is something one creates.***"**
>
> —⟶ THOMAS SZASZ

"He needed to find himself," we say about someone who went through the proverbial midlife crisis. What is there to find? We carry our truest self with us wherever we go. Traveling and trying new things can spark our creativity and help us understand ourselves better, but we don't need to go anywhere to start the daily work of creating a healthy self.

More productive than any drastic lifestyle change or spontaneous purchase, acts of listening are how we begin the process of creating ourselves. Then we can build, block-by-block, the self we crave.

I don't need to go somewhere extravagant to find myself. I can begin creating and re-creating myself by pausing to listen wherever I am right now. As I listen, I will discover the first step I can take on a new path.

Security is a myth

"Security is mostly superstition. It does not exist in nature."

—⌐ HELEN KELLER

We want to feel safe, and it's good and healthy for us to have relationships and home space in which we do. But, it can be limiting to require a perfect sense of security everywhere we go. Life is uncertain, and much of what we get to do with our lives is make decisions about how to best manage risks—not avoid them. Each day we get out of bed, we begin our interaction with risk. Once we accept that complete security is a myth, we can face life more honestly, viewing it as an unpredictable adventure. Instead of trying to control our lives, we can explore them.

I wish I could feel secure all the time, but life can be random. I will stay light on my feet, ready to respond to changes and surprises.

Reconciliation

"Reconciliation is more beautiful than victory."
—— VIOLETA BARRIOS DE CHAMORRO

When we get in an argument, our tunnel vision makes it feel like our goal is to win. We want the other person to give in and say we're right. But, a persuasive victory is rarely a boon to the relationship. Maybe we're right, maybe we're not. Maybe neither of us is right.

In the end, even if we're right, we don't really feel good about the situation unless the relationship is patched up. Even if we "win" the argument, we feel terrible if the other person is bitter or hurt. Reconciliation takes more time, thought, and kindness—and it is the only end that leaves us truly happy.

When I'm in an argument, I'll think twice about doing or saying anything that might make reconciliation difficult or impossible.

Intuition, then intellect

"I make all my decisions on intuition. I throw a
spear into the darkness. That is intuition. Then I
must send an army into the darkness to find the
spear. That is intellect."

—⌁ INGMAR BERGMAN

Some of the most successful people claim they
rarely wait to have all the facts lined up in order
to make a major decision. Instead, they seem to
track down the right path like a bloodhound.
They catch the trail and just know. Later on, the
facts and research come into play merely to confirm what they knew to be the right approach
all along.

Facts and statistics are good, but my hunches are
very powerful. I will listen to my intuition and
hone it by relying on it in my decision-
making process.

The art of waiting

"Waiting is one of the great arts."
—◇ MARGERY ALLINGHAM

"May my little girl listen to you practice violin?" a woman asked a young musician. "I'm trying to teach her that waiting quietly can be fun." What a pleasant thought. That toddler got a head start on learning an art quite forgotten—or never learned—by most adults.

Waiting is an art. It takes discipline to quiet our minds rather than reach for the next distraction, tapping our fingers in impatience. It's more satisfying, and even fun, to rest and let the moment be. We discover a hidden gift in the middle of the day: a chance to come back into our selves and be aware of only this moment.

The next time I'm in a line waiting, instead of reaching for headphones or a magazine, I'll simply wait without creating any distractions for myself.

Deal with anger

"I used to store my anger and it affected my play. Now I get it out. I'm never rude to my playing partner. I'm very focused on the ball. Then it's over."

— HELEN ALFREDSSON

Stuffing our anger isn't a good way to deal with it. "Oh, it's no big deal," we tell others. "I'm fine." Even when it's not true.

There are ways to express anger. In the safest relationships, we should be able to say we feel angry about something, but sometimes the other person isn't ready to handle it. We may need to wait until later and then release our feelings through athletic activity or artistic expression. Surprisingly, once we commit to expressing anger, it may take very little time before it dissipates.

There are appropriate ways for me to express anger. Whatever the situation, I will find the best way for me to deal with it, so I can move on.

Downsizing

" Transformation also means looking for ways to stop pushing yourself so hard professionally or inviting so much stress. "

—ᘒ GAIL SHEEHY

We may think of personal transformation in terms of goal-setting and then reaching our dreams. That involves a lot of work. Transformation can just as easily refer to downsizing our lives and our schedules. Sometimes our healthiest goal is to slow down, to be more present with our loved ones, to breathe. That kind of downsizing may be hard to measure, but vital as we create and re-create our lives.

Improving myself doesn't always mean adding more to an already full plate. Sometimes—maybe quite often—it means taking several things off my plate.

Thought for others

"Be unselfish . . . If you think of yourself only, you cannot develop because you are choking the source of development, which is spiritual expansion through thought for others."

— CHARLES W. ELIOT

If self-awareness is an integral part of spiritual development, awareness of others is its close companion. They balance each other and propel us forward. Too focused on ourselves, we can grow miserable operating with only our own energy and insight. Too focused on others, we grow codependent, needing them to give us identity.

We grow by balancing our own needs with those of others. We take care of ourselves, but live a rich life of service and love.

If I get too focused on myself, I start to feel drained, even when I'm not giving much. Maybe the best thing I can do is a small caring act for someone else. It might make their day, and it will help me get out of my own rut.

No perfect answer

*" True freedom lies in the realization and calm
acceptance of the fact that there may very well
be no perfect answer. "*

— A L L E N R E I D M C G I N N I S

Our decisions are not always tidy. There are
loose ends. There are wants and needs unmet.
We make a compromise. That's okay. Whether
we're looking for the perfect job or working
through a family conflict, we experience situations in which we cannot all get our own way at
the same time. Our life here is not Utopian. It is
collaborative though, and that can be satisfying.

When I accept there is not going to be an answer
that makes everyone 100 percent happy, I free
myself to consider a multitude of options
for compromise.

Forgive all, every night

> *"One of the secrets of a long and fruitful life is to forgive everybody everything every night before you go to bed."*
>
> — ANONYMOUS

To hold grudges only hurts us in the long run. When we go to bed mulling over an injustice, we sleep poorly. Sometimes we wake up thinking the same sequence of bitter thoughts, as if we never stopped wrestling with the matter. We don't feel rested, and that further contributes to our bad attitude. Compounded over years, this cycle of anger and bitterness can hold us back from the good life we want.

We can choose to end that cycle. Our choice to forgive does more for us than for the one we are forgiving. In letting go, we feel the tension in our shoulders relax. Our thoughts soften. We rest.

I let go of any bitterness I have right now and forgive those who have wronged me.

Conformity . . . or not

> ❝ *To know what you prefer, instead of humbly saying Amen to what the world tells you that you ought to prefer, is to have kept your soul alive.* ❞
> —⟡ ROBERT LOUIS STEVENSON

*I*t takes work to get ourselves out of autopilot. There are many ways we can just keep going along in pre-packaged lives. How rich life becomes when we step out of the predictable in order to examine our personal needs, talents, and desires. Then we craft a life based on what we've discovered. Where do we really want to live? Work? Play? Interact? How can we get there? The moment we take those questions seriously, a dormant part of us comes alive.

Instead of doing only what is expected, I will ask and personally wrestle with answering the hard questions about my life.

Honest attention

"A sense of duty is useful in work, but offensive in personal relations. People wish to be liked, not endured with patient resignation."

— BERTRAND RUSSELL

Our demeanor says it all as we look at our watch while a friend tries to finish a thought. We take time to be with someone who is going through something difficult, but we don't really listen. It's no fun to have a conversation with someone who is tapping their fingers in impatience or who appears too busy to listen when we try to tell them something.

When life has gotten too full of obligations for us to be fully present with people, it's time for an attitude change. We are missing out on true connection with others. People are intrinsically valuable and deserve our full, caring attention.

I will be careful to be present with the person who is talking to me and focus on how precious they are.

Handle with care

"Good friendships are fragile things and require as much care as any other fragile and precious thing."

—— Randolph Bourne

We often give more courtesy and gentle regard to total strangers than we do to our closest intimates. It's strange and sad that those dearest to us are the ones we take for granted. We let our poor manners and disrespect hang out around them. We should not require our loved ones to tolerate a lack of care on our behalf. We can build great trust with each other when we act with utmost respect and care.

I will treat my friends and loved ones with attentive care, handling them gently and keeping them in high regard.

One life to live

❝Most of us spend our lives as if we had another one in the bank.❞

—◌ BEN IRWIN

There is only one life we can influence and guide—the one we're living right now. Regardless, we often waste time or spend it poorly. We may fashion a budget that reflects our beliefs and values; we can do the same with our lifestyle and schedules. We need to check in with ourselves occasionally to see whether we're budgeting our lives appropriately.

How do we spend our days? What is our attitude? Is our lifestyle aligned with our beliefs? Answering those questions, we can adjust as needed, ensuring that we live our lives well and thoughtfully.

I can only make choices that influence my life as I live it right now. I will be mindful how I use my time and affect my surroundings.

Eliminate nonessentials

> *The wisdom of life consists in the elimination of nonessentials.*
>
> —⌘ LIN YUTANG

"Keep it simple," we advise each other. Easier said than done in today's world. So many distractions, so little time. Regardless of our religious persuasion, we are spiritual creatures. The rush and hurry and all the wonderful stuff— none of this makes us truly happy. It is wise to cut back and reduce the elements that make up our lives. From the size and contents of our home to the commitments on our calendars, we can prune our lifestyle to a healthy size that leaves more room for our spirits to grow.

I recognize the nonessentials in my life right now. I will trim some back and be mindful about continuing to protect my life from too many distractions.

All good things

> *"Fear less, hope more; eat less, chew more; whine less, breathe more; talk less, say more; love more, and all good things will be yours."*
>
> —⟶ SWEDISH PROVERB

We know the feeling of imbalance in our lives. We feel rushed and frustrated, as if there will never be enough. We give way to worry and it affects everything we do. Time to slow down; we have what we need. We can be present in each moment and come back to the center of love. When we live and act out of love—love for ourselves and for others—we discover a slower, healthier, more attentive pace.

I've gotten this far in life, and I've learned that somehow there's always enough. I will slow down, take a deep breath, and let myself enjoy each moment.

Simplify, simplify

*"A man must be able to cut a knot, for everything
cannot be untied; he must know how to disengage
what is essential from the detail in which it is
enwrapped, for everything cannot be equally
considered; in a word, he must be able to simplify
his duties, his business, and his life."*

—HENRI FREDERIC AMIEL

We've all had the feeling that we're hitting the
same brick wall, over and over. Finally, we have
the presence of mind to look creatively at the
situation. There is a simple remedy to the problem. "Oh, why didn't I think of that earlier?" we
ask ourselves.

We can set the stage for thinking those wise
thoughts sooner. It starts with a lifestyle that
includes taking time to breathe and simply *be*.
If we take an attitude of simplicity each day,
creative solutions will be readily available when
we need them.

I will maintain a daily attitude of peace so I can
approach challenges with serenity.

Joy sees beauty in everything

> *"All times are beautiful for those who maintain joy within them; but there is no happy or favorable time for those with disconsolate or orphaned souls."*
>
> — ROSALIA CASTRO

A blue attitude really does color everything. Nothing can make us happy when we're depressed; even our favorite activities seem dull or downright discouraging. Conversely, a joyful spirit will find delight in even the smallest pleasure.

There are appropriate times for grief and sadness, but we are meant to grow through those times, not stay in them. Caring for ourselves gently, we can travel through the blue time and begin to lay hold of joy again.

My attitude colors how I view everything in my life. When I am joyful, I can find cause for joy all around me. During very sad times, it seems nothing can make me happy. I will continue my upward climb toward joy.

Don't wait for inspiration

"We should be taught not to wait for inspiration to start a thing. Action always generates inspiration. Inspiration seldom generates action."

— FRANK TIBOLT

Sometimes we think, "I'd like to do that some-day, but I'm waiting for some real inspiration." Inspiration comes so rarely, though, and the great idea is postponed indefinitely.

People who complete creative work often say that inspiration is important, but it can't be the sole impetus behind any big project. The most important factor is simply showing up and doing one small task on a regular basis. Inspiration comes when we get in the habit of making the dedicated time for it to come.

I've been waiting for inspiration to begin work on a great idea I have. Instead of waiting any longer, I will set aside time to get started and see what happens.

Repose

"When the heart is at ease, the body is healthy."
— CHINESE PROVERB

Soul and body are intertwined. Serious, prolonged stress can compromise the immune system and aggravate any health problems we have. Likewise, when we are living a meaningful and centered life and keeping our integrity, we are able to rest well and our physical systems work a little more smoothly.

Science is just beginning to discover the ways in which a rich spiritual life can affect our biochemistry, sleep, hormones, and immune response. Even without knowing the exact "how," we can enjoy the effects.

The state of my spiritual heart may have an effect on my body. Making decisions with personal integrity and cultivating my spiritual life is an important part of my overall health.

Houseguests

"Fish and houseguests go bad in three days."
—— SWEDISH PROVERB

Our lives feel full when family or friends from out of town stay with us, or we travel to stay with them. The house is warm with constant activity and conversation as we catch up on each other's lives and enjoy sightseeing and eating together. We should remember it's only natural that sharing the house, kitchen, and bathroom, can become stressful for everyone involved, even when we care for each other.

Three days may not be quite enough time to be together, but it's good to think about the temperaments and habits of everyone involved and plan a visit that respects them.

Whether I am excited or a little apprehensive about an upcoming visit, things will go more smoothly if I gently make my needs and expectations known in advance.

A flock of friends

"*Fortify yourself with a flock of friends! You can select them at random, write to one, dine with one, visit one, or take your problems to one. There is always at least one who will understand, inspire, and give you the lift you may need at the time.*"

—⟋ GEORGE MATTHEW ADAMS

Chances are, we have a few close friends whom we depend on as confidants. It's great to surround that inner circle with a larger group of diverse friendships, too. When we have many friends in that second tier, we always have someone to go to. With a diverse social group, we can enjoy a wider range of activities, opinions, and conversation topics.

I will grow and care for a wide group of casual friendships. Whether I feel like working out, eating a fine meal, or talking politics, I'll always know there is someone I can call for a little companionship.

A lamp should shine

"No one lights a lamp and hides it in a jar or puts it under a bed. Instead, he puts it on a stand, so that those who come in can see the light."

—JESUS

Our stories of faith and the spiritual lessons we've learned are valuable. That learning has become a guiding light for us. The deepest truths are beacons that will continue to help us in many situations in the future. We should not be shy about pointing out those beacons for others, too; perhaps they'll avoid some of the mistakes we made or find encouragement to act in faith at a time when they are feeling afraid. We can help by sharing our stories and letting others draw their own conclusions.

There are many important spiritual truths I've learned over the years. I will not be afraid to graciously share one of those truths when it seems that someone might benefit from it.

Rest and labor

"Put off thy cares with thy clothes; so shall thy rest strengthen thy labor, and so thy labor sweeten thy rest."

—⁊ FRANCIS QUARLES

Whether we're worrying or just pondering pleasant memories, sometimes our body seems to have no interest in sleeping. We may calm the mind if we visualize folding up each thought like a garment and putting it away, promising ourselves that we can take it up again in the morning when the time is right.

Waking up rested, we're able to work at a better pace and get a little exercise without fighting to stay awake. Then, when we're naturally spent from a full day, tiredness comes. When in proper balance, labor and rest can support each other beautifully.

I relinquish all my cares and welcome sleep. I will work hard tomorrow and welcome the peaceful evening again when the day comes to a close.

New habits

"*To learn new habits is everything, for it is to reach the substance of life. Life is but a tissue of habits.*"

—<small>Henri Frederic Amiel</small>

Habits are outward expressions of our beliefs. No wonder they can be hard to change. We often need to revise a belief or set of beliefs before we can change, stop, or add a habit.

If we don't think we have the self-control or ability to change, that's the belief we need to work on before we can begin to change a habit. When we successfully learn a new habit, we affirm that we are able to change, that we can improve ourselves. A new habit is the doorway to change.

I am able to learn new positive habits. I will look for any personal beliefs that have held me back from change in the past and then choose a better belief.

Pleasant memories

❝*God gave us memory that we might have roses in December.*❞

— ⌁ SIR JAMES M. BARRIE

Even on the coldest winter day, we can remember a time of balmy warmth and beautiful flowers. On hot days, we take comfort in recalling cooler seasons. Whatever our present challenge, trial, or grief, we can look back to a friendlier time and take comfort in the memory. If things were better once, they will be again.

I have many different memories. I will treasure the pleasant ones as touchstones I can go to for encouragement and inspiration.

Mistakes lead to success

*"The error of the past is the success of the future.
A mistake is evidence that someone tried to
do something."*

—⊂ ANONYMOUS

I feels safe to keep things as they are. Those willing to take a risk are trying to adjust things for the better. Life becomes an experiment when we open the door to change and invention. It's inevitable that some attempts end in failure, but failures are always instructive. We figure out why something didn't work and then make further adjustments. Eventually, trial and error lead to success.

I'm not afraid of making mistakes. In fact, I welcome them. Mistakes can show me how to proceed.

Speaking to the subconscious

> *"The first thing each morning, and the last thing each night, suggest to yourself specific ideas that you wish to embody in your character and personality. Address such suggestions to yourself, silently or aloud, until they are deeply impressed upon your mind."*
>
> — GRENVILLE KLEISER

The semi-wakeful minutes immediately before and just after sleep are powerful moments. These are the only pockets of time when we can purposely influence the workings of our subconscious.

When we speak affirmations to ourselves at these times, they can take root, re-wiring our thought patterns and creating new beliefs about ourselves. When that work is successful, we see it manifest in surprising changes during our waking hours.

If there's something I'm trying to change in my life, I'll write a positive affirmation about it, then read that sentiment each night and each morning.

The value of artistry

> "*Non-cooks think it's silly to invest two hours' work in two minutes' enjoyment; but if cooking is evanescent, so is the ballet.*"
>
> —◦ JULIA CHILD

We need room for self-expression and creativity. Whether we cook, dance, paint, or write, we are involved in the business of being human. Creativity is at the core of who we are, even if we do not see ourselves as artistic types. Creativity that gives us a fleeting experience is no less an art form than those that create lasting items. Any art we experience can live long in our memories.

Perhaps it does not seem pragmatic to spend two hours preparing a fine meal. But, as a sincere expression of the soul, that meal is a touchstone for its maker's creativity and humanity.

I don't fully understand all the arts and hobbies that people enjoy, but I do appreciate the spark of creativity they all have in common.

True courage

> *"Courage is rarely reckless or foolish . . . courage usually involves a highly realistic estimate of the odds that must be faced."*
>
> —*&* MARGARET TRUMAN

Courage is not equivalent to bravado or grandiosity, even if movies make it look that way. Courage in the real world is humble. "I did what anyone with my training would have done," the real-life hero states. "I saw what was possible, and I did it."

A courageous person often admits to being afraid—they knew there was risk. But they took every precaution they could and did what they believed was right. Although the thought process may take place in the blink of an eye, true courage comes from understanding the situation, evaluating risk, and deciding how to proceed in the face of fear.

Being courageous doesn't mean I would take up an extreme sport. Real courage simply means doing the right thing—even when it scares me.

Another door opens

> ❝*When one door closes another opens. But we often look so long and so regretfully upon the closed door that we fail to see the one that has opened for us.*❞
>
> —ᴄᴏ ALEXANDER GRAHAM BELL

Lingering in our regret is self-defeating. When we lose an opportunity or it becomes clear that a certain plan will not work, it's disappointing, but we need not be consumed by the loss. There are other possibilities. Perhaps we've overlooked an option. Perhaps someone we know has a great idea. We can take all that energy we might have given to disappointment and use it to begin searching for the other open door. We will notice it sooner if our gaze is up and our attitude expectant.

It's fine to feel disappointed when something doesn't work out, but I need to keep my antenna up and alert to alternatives.

Giving

❝ *Think of giving not as a duty but as a privilege.* ❞

—⌘ JOHN D. ROCKEFELLER, JR.

In our consumer culture, we are bombarded with advertising messages about the perfect gift, or the "must-have" item for the holidays. The pressure to surprise and delight our loved ones sometimes leaves us feeling anxious, harried, and resenting the amount of time, money, and energy we're spending as we run from store to store.

Real giving—of our hearts, if not our money—should never feel like an onerous duty. When we bring a smile to a child's face or tears of joy to the eyes of a loved one, we are reminded of how fortunate we are to live and love. By giving to others, we are bestowing a gift unto ourselves.

This season, I will give from my heart—recognizing what a privilege it is to touch the lives of others.

Person to person

"Do not wait for leaders; do it alone, person to person."

——⌇ MOTHER TERESA

We can complain about how things are and how we need better leadership. But we can be a more powerful force by starting the change ourselves. What do we want to see more of in our world? Compassion, innovation, friendship, creativity, profit, conservation—we can offer these in small ways ourselves.

I wonder how I can make the change that I want to see in my world. I can take a small action this week.

The body is a temple

"*Every man is the builder of a temple called his body.*"

—◌ HENRY DAVID THOREAU

Many spiritual traditions refer to the body as a temple, either individually or collectively. Wherever we go, our bodies are testimonies to the way we live. They are visual expressions of our inner beliefs. This raw material is a precious gift; it is our privilege to treat it with care, intention, and dedication.

I am grateful for my body. I will listen to what it needs and care for it as a spiritual act of gratitude.

Multi-tasking

"He who hunts two hares, leaves one and loses the other."

——⌒ JAPANESE PROVERB

We strive to be as efficient as possible, making our moments work double- or even triple-time. Yet, we are all familiar with the sting and disappointment of divided attention. At work and home, it hurts to be the recipient of halfhearted listening and shortcuts.

Becoming too focused on getting everything done quickly can complicate things. Balancing a handful of tasks at once, we forget important details and make mistakes. Perhaps it's time to adjust a little.

There are some relationships that have been hurt by my hurried pace. I have the time to focus on the individual person or task entrusted to me in each moment.

Discovered talent

" *We are told that talent creates its own opportunities. But it sometimes seems that intense desire creates not only its own opportunities, but its own talents.* "

— ERIC HOFFER

Driven by a cause, or a sense of higher purpose, it is amazing what we can achieve. It is equally amazing what lengths we will go to learn a new skill that is essential to our success. Convinced that a message needs to get out, we lose our fear of public speaking and discover we are solid writers. Hoping to connect better with a loved one, we find out we have a natural aptitude for one of their favorite sports and can share the activity with them.

The main ingredients, in addition to desire, are a willingness to try and the recognition that we may discover something new about ourselves.

I am open to discovering my hidden talents. I permit myself to try something completely new.

Understanding brings peace

> ❝*I do not want the peace which passeth understanding, I want the understanding which bringeth peace.*❞
>
> —◦ HELEN KELLER

Well-founded peace is unshakable. It takes work and discovery to develop that level of peace. The unknown always seems a little scary. Anxiety, frustration, and fear often stem from lacking a full understanding of a situation or relationship. The discontent can also come from our own unhealed hurts.

Whether we seek to better understand other people and situations or to learn more about our own personal needs and healing processes, the natural by-product of increased understanding is greater peace.

I recognize there are areas in my life that lack peace. I will look for ways to increase my understanding so the unknown no longer seems so intimidating.

Unshakeable peace

"*If you do not find peace in yourself, you will never find it anywhere else.*"

— PAULA A. BENDRY

By definition, inner peace is a state of rest, unshakeable by external circumstances. We may look for peace by trying to make our surroundings more pleasant. But, if we are in a peaceful room or moment, it's likely we are not experiencing internal peace so much as contentment with what's around us. The hallmark of peace is its existence in the middle of a frustrating or frightening situation.

Once we've experienced that real peace, we are able to enter into that state a little more easily the next time a tricky challenge arises. We're able to appreciate the contented moments even more, too!

I am grateful for the chances to practice unshakeable peace.

A kind response

❝ *Be kind, for everyone you meet is fighting a hard battle.* ❞

—✐ PLATO

Things are rarely what they seem. Often, we can defuse a tense situation by listening to the other, asking questions, and exploring from where the tension may be coming.

In passing moments, when we haven't time to discover those details, kindness is still a wise response. Not a passive rolling over or giving in, the kind word in the face of an uncomfortable interaction comes from a place of strength. It alters the atmosphere and disarms most attacks.

I will watch for the opportunity to practice kindness in difficult encounters.

Photo credits:

"A Fond Farewell" (p. 399), "Discovery Park Lighthouse II (with Yellow Flowers)" (p. 153), "Laguna Beach Sunset" (p. 352), "Red Rocks II" (p. 103), "Starfish Love Sunsets Too" (p. 247), and "Twilight Delight" (p. 45) © Darien Chin.

"Balestrand, Norway" (p. 198) and "Whisky Cave, Isle of Mull" (p. 167) © Steve Deger.

"Late Again" (p. 304), "Midnight Conversation" (p. 363), and "Silk River" (p. 127) © James Gallimore.

"Anomaly" (p. 81), "Connect" (p. 315), "Continuum" (p. 388), "Halo" (p. 92), "Infinity and Beyond" (p. 11), "Lavendar Coast" (p. 176), "Perpetual Flow" (p. 122), "Pyro" (p. 260), "Shoal" (p. 273), "Silk" (p. 327), "Starburst" (p. 56), and "Wave" (p. 140) © Anthony James.

"Dusk" (p. 24), "From Me to You" (p. 33), "Make A Wish" (p. 116), "Spooky" (p. 340), and "The Sky is the Limit" (p. 283) © Dian Karlina.

"Moonlight at Rondeau Park" (p. 187) and "Sunset at the Yacht Club" (p. 235) © Bob West.

"Flowing Sand, Antelope Canyon" (p. 68), "Golden Gate, by Moonlight" (p. vii), "Pigeon Point Lighthouse" (p. 211), and "Sunset at Rodeo Lagoon" (p. 375) © Tyler Westcott.